HEARTH
OF
DARKNESS

HEARTH OF DARKNESS

IF YOUR HOME HAD A DARK PAST,
WOULD YOU WANT TO KNOW?

MATT BLAKE

Elliott&Thompson

First published 2025 by
Elliott and Thompson Limited
2 John Street
London WC1N 2ES
www.eandtbooks.com

Represented by:
Authorised Rep Compliance Ltd
Ground Floor, 71 Lower Baggot Street
Dublin, D02 P593
Ireland
www.arccompliance.com

ISBN: 978-1-78396-915-9

9 8 7 6 5 4 3 2 1

A catalogue record for this book is available from
the British Library.

Typesetting: Marie Doherty
Printed by CPI Group (UK) Ltd, Croydon, CR0 4YY

For Jasmine

One need not be a chamber—to be haunted—
One need not be a House—
The Brain—has Corridors surpassing
Material Place—

Emily Dickinson (1830–86)

CONTENTS

PROLOGUE

The night curled around my house without sound. Its cold fingers ran up the facade and along the sills, slipping in through the windows and stroking the walls. Shadows pooled in the corners as if they'd been waiting all day. Only the old sycamore outside resisted the dark's silence with a whisper.

I was in a deep sleep, lost in the oblivion of total exhaustion. The move had been taxing, both physically and emotionally, and I had collapsed into bed grateful to put another day behind me. This house, with its creaking boards and battered walls, was supposed to be a fresh start after a sticky divorce – a place that was quiet and safe, where I could heal and my daughter could grow.

Through the darkness came a voice.

'Daaaaadddyyyy.'

It sounded faint, as if coming from next door, or in the street. I rolled over.

It came again.

'Daddyyyy, where are yooouuu?'

It was much clearer now, and louder, wafting up from what sounded like downstairs. My mind straightened, and I realised: it was Jasmine's voice.

'I'm in bed,' I called back. 'Come in here. What's wrong?'

I heard her footsteps on the stairs, then three creaks on the landing. The door opened. She stood there, silhouetted by moonlight, squeezing Bunny the toy rabbit, who hadn't left her side since the separation.

'I had scary dream, and I woke up,' her voice wobbled. 'Then, the radio was talking downstairs. I went to find you. But you weren't there. I thought you left me by myself.'

I checked my phone. 5.23 a.m.

'I've been here the whole time,' I said, trying to sound soothing. 'The radio wasn't on, love. You must've dreamed it.'

'It *iiis*,' she replied. 'Downstairs.'

The radio downstairs was a digital DAB plug-in that my new girlfriend, Jody, had given me for my birthday a month earlier. But I hadn't used it today, nor any other day for at least the past week. I knew this because today was Tuesday, and I'd been at Jody's all weekend while Jasmine was at her mum's. So, there was no possible way it could be on right now.

Jasmine had climbed into my bed, and was already under the covers, snuggling up to Bunny. 'It's on now,' she repeated, her voice drifting. 'Very loud . . .'

I had to check for myself.

I swung my feet out of bed and felt a chill on my skin. I put on my dressing gown and took a step towards the door. Jasmine grabbed my arm. 'Don't go, Daddy. I'm scared.' I looked at her and felt a pang of guilt. The divorce, I knew, had been hard on her. She needed me now more than ever.

I kissed her forehead. 'It's okay. I'll be right back. I just need to see what's going on with the radio. Nothing to worry about.' I was trying to sound brave. How could the radio be on when I hadn't touched it in days? Was someone in the house? I opened my bedside drawer and took out my 'emergencies' hammer – the one I'd stashed in case a fox climbed in through an open window. Or a homicidal drifter. I left the room and crept down the stairs, which seemed to creak louder with every step.

Then . . . *Hang on, is that . . .?* I could hear music drifting up the house. It was soft at first. But it grew louder as I descended.

Confused and groggy, I tried to anchor myself back to reality, straining my ears through the darkness. I knew the song. It was 'Mis-Shapes' by Pulp, one of my favourite bands from the nineties – a bouncy, catchy battle cry for suburban outcasts of the past, and a completely inappropriate soundtrack, I thought, for my imminent murder. But it sounded distorted, as if the signal was breaking up. Still, I could hear the lyrics – about taking people's homes and people's lives. I knew them well.

I was alone on the stairs. Yet, suddenly, I felt a tingling sense of being watched. The house's shadows seemed so thick and black as they coiled around my mind, drawing me towards them. I squeezed the hammer and pushed the door ajar with my foot. My heartbeat was thumping the inside of my skull. I peered inside. The room was dark, except for a trickle of watery moonlight leaking in through the blinds. My eye followed the light across the room to the mantelpiece. There, cast in white, I could make out the faint glow of the radio display, exactly where I had left it. It was plugged in, and the display showed the time, the station name and the song title. Everything else was in shadow. I scanned the room for movement. Nothing. Pulp had finished and a presenter was now gibbering about the nation's favourite sandwiches, asking listeners to ring in with theirs. Something by Bruce Springsteen came on.

I reached out my hand and turned it off, filling the room with a silence you could spread on toast, thickened by the slow tick-tock of the mantelpiece clock. I stood rooted to the old floorboards. I was too frightened to look around the room. It was so dark and so quiet. I just listened. I was sure I felt a breath on the nape of my neck.

'Hello?' I called out, unheroically.

No sound. I was definitely alone. But I couldn't shake the feeling that I wasn't. Fear does strange things to the brain. It may sound like the tired, under-examined anxieties of a grown man who can't admit he's still afraid of the dark, but the house seemed to breathe around me, as though it was whispering dark somethings in a language I couldn't understand.

That is when I saw something move in the corner of my eye. My head snapped towards the open doorway that led to the kitchen at the back of the house. *Was there someone at the window? Was that . . . Could it be . . . Did a figure flash past the black glass outside?* I peered into the darkness until my eyes felt dry, but all I could see was my own waxy reflection squinting back at me.

Had Jasmine been playing a prank? Impossible. The radio was too high up on the mantelpiece for her to reach. I fumbled about with the buttons until I found the alarm settings, which I'd never used before. None of them was set. A power surge maybe, I thought. But wouldn't that have reset the oven clock? I could see from where I was that its display panel wasn't blinking, so that could not be the answer.

With a shiver, I retreated back to my room, those lyrics still echoing in my ears. But I didn't fall back to sleep. How could I sleep?

Lying in the darkness with Jasmine beside me, I suddenly became as easily startled as a child. The car alarm in the distance, a neighbour slamming shut a front door, the pigeon flapping at the window. I found myself peering around the bedroom, checking shadows were in the same place that they had been the night before.

There had to be a perfectly reasonable explanation, I told myself. But what if there wasn't? What if the house itself was trying to communicate, using its own cryptic language, a language of creaks and groans, of electrical pulses and shifting shadows? The thought was unsettling, yet strangely compelling. I knew from the deeds it was an old house. And like all old houses, maybe this one held stories, not just in its walls, but in – as the ancient Romans called it – its *genius loci*. Its very essence.

When it is warm and the sun is out, I'll tell you I don't believe in ghosts. I don't believe in auras or chakras or guardian angels or third eyes or 'old souls'. No thanks, never have. But I do believe in the brain's woeful inadequacies when it comes to processing the vast ocean of electromagnetic radiation that surrounds us. Very little about reality is exactly what it appears. The human eye, for instance, can perceive less than a ten-trillionth of the light spectrum.[1] Like children peering through a keyhole, we see, hear, and feel only what our limited senses allow us to, while the rest – a sprawling, unseen universe of wonders and terrors – lies just beyond our grasp, in darkness and silence.

I've lived in more than a dozen homes over the years, and I'd never had a radio that turned itself on. I resolved that, in the morning, I would do what any sane person would do and Google it. The internet would have the answer.

Finally, I drifted into a thin and dreamless sleep, those haunting lyrics still bouncing about my brain.

Chapter 1

FINDING HOME

Everyone knows the first thing you do when you move into a new house is wipe all memory of the previous owners,' said my younger brother Nick, toeing a dent in the carpet where someone else's bed had once stood. 'It's fucking dreadful, Matthew.'

Nick calls me Matthew when he wants to sound authoritative – a middle-brother thing. I have two brothers who are my best friends. But, like all brothers, each knows exactly where the others keep the kryptonite. Nick must have noticed the stink eye I flashed him across the room because he then clarified: 'Not the house. I like the house. I mean this carpet. It's got to go.'

It was January 2021 and, eighteen months after my divorce, I'd finally bought a house. I bought it partly because I could – after ten years together, my ex-wife Lisa and I had got lucky on the property ladder and walked away with enough money for a deposit each. But also, I bought it because I was desperate. With shared custody of a four-year-old daughter, I needed a place where she could be happy, and where I could get back on my feet.

For those first few weeks, this house was far from a home. It was more a collection of empty rooms decorated only by the telltale hints of lives gone by. The walls were bare apart from a few ghostly rectangles where someone else's pictures had once hung. The stairs creaked from a century of footsteps. Even the toilet was caked with a thick crust of another family's limescale. And despite the best efforts of the old boiler downstairs, the house was strangely chilly, lifeless, as if waiting for a child's laugh or a clatter of pots and pans or the familiar melody of a morning routine – any sign of life to bring warmth to this place again.

Nick wasn't wrong about the carpet. We were standing in the main bedroom, to the front of the property, and the carpet was as grotty as any I'd seen. It wasn't just its greasy feel underfoot that bothered us. It was the colour – a sort of browny-grey that suits an elephant, but never a bedroom floor.

'You might say it's the . . .' I paused for dramatic effect '. . . elephant in the room.'

Nick rolled his eyes in the way only a younger brother knows how. 'Come on,' he said. 'I'll start in that corner, you start over there.'

At first, the carpet clung to the floor like a stubborn child. So, we enlisted the help of 'The Persuader' – or, as it's known to everyone else, Nick's hammer. It made a convincing argument, and, after some cajoling, the carpet grudgingly gave way, revealing the floor beneath.

Suddenly, Nick stopped yanking and stood up.

'There's something wrong with your boards,' he said, squinting at his feet. 'Is it . . .' He tilted his head to the left, then to the right, puzzled. 'Is it a stain?'

The more we pulled, the more we saw. Inch by inch, an amorphous patch of black began to bleed out across the centre of the room like a giant Rorschach test for anxious new homeowners.

'You know, I've read that dead bodies leave stains like that,' Nick exhaled, a sardonic smile playing on his lips. 'Cadaver juice, I reckon. Dead man's ooze.'

For a moment, his gallows humour swung in the air between us. In the darkest spots there were hand-sized holes in the floorboards through which we could see radiator pipes and dusty old 1970s beer cans left behind by workmen of the past. Some of the boards appeared chewed up, deformed, and peppered by flecks of white and grey.

Then it dawned on us. 'There's been a fire here,' said Nick, more grimly this time. 'A big one. You think someone fell asleep in bed with a cigarette?'

—

Two weeks earlier, I was sitting alone downstairs, on the empty floor of my new living room, wondering how many slugs it takes to make an omen. Looking back, perhaps they were an omen. A three-strong phlegm of them was slithering towards me across the empty floor, welcoming me to my new home.

I had a celebratory can of Carlsberg in one hand and the house keys the estate agent had given me in the other. I'd not bought any furniture yet so it was just me and the slugs, casting figures of eight in mucus up the walls and across the peeling wood-effect laminate floor. From certain angles, the trails looked strangely beautiful when they caught the light.

'It's you and me now,' I thought out loud, raising the Carlsberg and realising immediately how stupid it was to be talking to a house.

The sun outside was fading, causing the shadows inside to

deepen. This gave the room a gloomier feel than I remembered from the sales viewing six months back. But the place had all the previous owners' stuff in it back then – sofas, curtains, house-plants, pictures. Now that was all gone, it looked so . . . old. It was as if the house's makeup that seduced me in the summer had been scrubbed off, exposing all the wrinkles and rough edges, the wear and tear of over a hundred years of occupancy. I could hear the boiler groaning petulantly while producing no heat at all. I could see a patch of mould creeping up the uPVC bay window. I could smell damp.

—

The divorce had hurt. There'd been no emotional or physical abuse in our marriage. No affairs. Love just curdled. Looking back, I don't blame her for ending the marriage. It hadn't aged well. And she was right: I could've been better. We both could.

We'd met at university ten years earlier. There was an instant attraction, and youthful passion quickly turned into sonnet-grade love. After graduation, I set out to become a journalist and landed my first job on the graduate scheme of a national newspaper in London. She was chasing work in fashion and grafted through a string of dressmaking jobs in various design studios before setting up a successful business teaching women how to make their own clothes. We moved in together after about four years, renting a small flat in Highbury near the old Arsenal stadium.

By then, landlords had easily slipped below estate agents, law-yers and journalists in the league of least-trusted professions on Earth, reaping the rewards of an economy built on a ballooning property market. Rents were soaring, while even one-bed flats near the centre of the capital were being sold for telephone-number prices. Buying a house inside the M25 had come to be regarded as an act only for the most privileged – or lucky – of our society. In a way we were both.

Of course we had help. You couldn't buy a house in London back then without help. In our case, the death of a grandparent left us with enough money for a small deposit, so long as we pooled our incomes to take on a mammoth mortgage. We were also helped, I'm not proud to admit, by the 2008 financial crash a few years earlier. It had led to a 20 per cent drop in property prices, leaving many homeowners in negative equity. On the other hand, it left renters like us with a rare opportunity to get a first foot on the housing ladder.

We took it. And in 2013, we bought our first flat together – a top-floor two-bed that overlooked a busy high street in East London and shuddered every time a bus drove past. A few years later Jasmine was born and our life together seemed mapped out: we had the mortgage and the baby; all that was left was to live happily ever after. The trouble started when we bought a bigger house.

'If you want to make money in property, you need to buy the ugliest house on the nicest street, and do it up,' an architect friend had told me. It felt like sound advice at the time. We sold the flat for exactly double what we'd paid, leaving us with enough of a deposit to buy a tumbledown terraced house on a leafy road by a canal, and secure a mortgage big enough to renovate.

The estate agent told us an old man had lived there for the past forty years since his wife had left him, taking their kids to another part of the country. I don't know his name, or what he looked like, only that he lived there alone, mostly in the front room. We later found out he'd become a hoarder in his twilight years, living among piles of newspapers, squashed cardboard boxes, surplus VHS recorders and radios, heaps of clothes and knick-knacks littering the stairs. He died in that front room, apparently, among his carefully curated corridors of personal arcana. Most of that had been removed when we arrived, leaving just the mouse-nibbled carpets, peeling wallpaper and a smell of impending sadness. Sadder still, he'd left the house to his ex-wife in his will. And now she wanted a quick sale.

I'd never seen a house more in need of renovation. So, we spent the next six months living among builders and dust and boxes, to the tune of banging and whirring and swearing in Albanian. And yet, the more beautiful the house became, the deeper our relationship fell into disrepair. Looking back, I'm still not exactly sure when it started. First it began to creak, and then to buckle. I've heard it said that the three most stressful life events (aside from grief and major illness) are: having a baby, renovating a house, getting divorced.

In our case, we'd achieved the first two by the age of thirty-five. We wouldn't need long to complete the set.

It wasn't that we hated each other. We'd simply grown apart. Petty annoyances, gone untreated, had spread into gaping patches of resentment. Where we used to just bicker, now we fought. Not like in movies – ours wasn't one of those relationships that went down in a hail of smashed plates and slammed doors. Just harsh truths spoken quietly, so as not to wake the baby.

—

Our marriage ended in a cafe on a busy road in Hackney.

'What about Jasmine?' I asked.

'In the long term, I don't know,' she said. 'She needs us both. But for now I think you should move out while we try to sell the house. We should take the money and buy our own places near enough to each other that we can divide her care equally.'

It takes a vast act of bravery to end a relationship after ten years and a baby. I know that now. And later, I came to respect her for doing what I never would have had the courage to do. When we got together, I realised, we were too young to know who we really were or what we wanted, and I think that scared us both to death. So we clung to each other for dear life. That worked for a time. But as life marched onwards, our relationship stayed still. By the end, the marriage had become an algorithm so convoluted with silly grudges and minor disappointments that its sums no longer added up.

And suddenly, the next thing you know we were in a cafe with buses roaring past and sun streaming in and tears in our eyes. Then our coffee cups were empty, and there was nothing more to say.

⁓

After we agreed that separation was our best option, we decided that she would stay in the house while I rented until we could find someone to buy it. Within a week of putting it on the market, a man in his early thirties who'd made his fortune in video games made an obscene offer. We split the profit in half, and Lisa immediately moved into a small house three miles up the road, across the Walthamstow marshes, in the borough of Waltham Forest, north-east London.

As for our daughter, there was never a question of how we'd divide her care. It would be fifty-fifty, the first half of the week spent at her mother's, the second half at mine. We would alternate weekends.

I knew I needed a place that was close enough to manage pickups and drop-offs, but not so close that we'd bump into each other in the pub. But more than that, I needed somewhere safe, somewhere sturdy – a house made of bricks that wouldn't blow away. So I focused my search on the other end of Walthamstow – not far from Markhouse Road, one of the main arteries in and out of the borough.

This part of Walthamstow is a staunchly residential area. Some houses are pebble-dashed. Some have doors painted in dusky pink or racing green. There are wind chimes, geraniums in boxes and the occasional cat sitting on a wheelie bin. Most streets have their own WhatsApp group so residents can share plumbers, grumble about 'bin day' or sound the alarm when a traffic warden is on the prowl. Running from Walthamstow Central to St James Street railway station is the longest open-air street market in Europe, where you can buy anything from four-foot cuddly teddy bears to sausage rolls the size of fists. It's a homely place.

Walthamstow, then, was not at all like Clapton, back over the marshes in the borough of Hackney. It had no boutique cake shops, mid-century vintage furniture stores or parody Instagram accounts. As a result, homes there were about half the price. They were also largely half the size. Most of the houses here were thrown up during its late-nineteenth-century industrial boom to house the families of workers relocating for jobs in the toy factories and garment warehouses springing up across the borough. But

Walthamstow had a new energy now. Almost every street had that unmistakable whiff of gentrification as a steady stream of middle-class families who couldn't afford to buy in Hackney poured in, building lofts and filling 'side returns', extending kitchens and putting solar panels on roofs. There was some resentment, and it was palpable in places. But where in London is that not the case?

Yes, south Walthamstow was right up my street.

By this time, a virus in China had turned into a plague and started killing people all over the world. Hospitals and morgues were at bursting point. People in England retreated inside, and when we did go out, we wore masks and only met in pairs. Computer screens became our windows on the world. Trousers had become optional.

Mind you, Covid-19 transformed Britain's relationship with indoor space. For many Londoners, it took being stuck at home through a pandemic to realise how important it was, and how little of it so many of us had.

So, when the first national lockdown ended in May 2020, the government bestowed a 'stamp-duty holiday' on home sales in a bid to revive the flagging housing market. It worked, and home-buying went berserk. Viewings were face-masked and frantic – a fifteen-minute speed date with a building to make the biggest financial decision of your life.

For me, that summer was a relentless blur of house viewings. I trudged from one property to the next, joining the throngs of hopeful buyers snaking along pavements and squeezing past each other in cramped hallways, all polite smiles masking simmering frustration. Couples, sometimes with babies in tow, curious in-laws, even anxious pets, added to the chaos. And then the silver-tongued estate agents in chinos and gilets saying things like, 'This home has so much character, it could practically write its own autobiography.'

But, after dozens of bumpy viewings, slippery sales agents and a couple of gazumped bids, I finally found it.

—

It wasn't my dream home. Unless you count anxiety dreams. But it ticked more boxes than it crossed. So, after a frazzling few months of paperwork, building surveys, mortgage applications and final price negotiations, at last we exchanged contracts. On a grey London day in January, towards the end of the third national lockdown, I got the keys. I was in.

In truth, I didn't remember much about the house from the viewing. So when I arrived on my first day as owner, turning the key over in my fingers, I peered up at the facade and bit my lip.

On a road lined by Victorian terraces, mine stood out like a cracked tooth. It had that hunched, worn, weathered look of a place that's taken its share of beatings over the years. It seemed to cower between its nicer neighbours, almost apologetically. The original bay window had been replaced with a uPVC box with a small porch. The brickwork had been covered in a thick white render that was now cracking like old makeup. Inside, the front room and dining area had been 'knocked through', and the stairs had been 'flipped' to the back of the house. The bathroom, once by the kitchen at the back, had been moved upstairs between two 'remodelled' bedrooms, one facing the street and one facing a petite garden with a lawn and a barren rose shrub.

And yet, despite all its scars and foibles, I had mixed emotions. On one side was a philharmonic string-section of elation and hope, accompanied on the other by a timpani of dread. Had I made a terrible mistake? No. Doubt was not an option. *I am the conductor of my life,* my brain repeatedly said to my nervous system. *I just have to make sure the violins play louder than the drums.*

I decided there and then that I would love this house with all my heart for the rest of my life – or its life, whichever was longer. This house represented a new start – a new future for both me and Jasmine.

The truth is, until I looked under that carpet, I never once thought about its past.

Chapter 2

THE MYSTERY OF THE BURNED FLOORBOARDS

All houses have histories. But how much thought do we give to what happened in them before we moved in? Like most people, I treated this house's past like the junk folder in my email: you know there might be bad stuff in there, but so long as you never open it, what harm can it do?

There are 27 million homes in England. The vast majority were built before 1980,[1] and a third of those, around 5 million, are more than a hundred years old. That's a lot of old homes; a lot of forgotten lives – their smells and noises now drowned out by time. It's a lot of secrets.

So, what happens when those secrets worm out – through layers of wallpaper, from beneath old wooden floorboards, stuffed up chimneys, wedged behind loose bricks, or from the mouths of gossiping neighbours? In my house's case, the scorched floorboards were just the beginning.

'We are delighted to present this excellently extended and refurbished two-bed terraced house,' the estate agent's listing had gushed. 'The property has been significantly improved by the current owners including an extension to the ground floor, providing a through reception room extending to over 24-feet and a separate, fitted kitchen.'

Having moved in, it quickly became clear the word 'excellently' and 'refurbished' were doing a lot of heavy lifting in that first sentence. So was the word 'improved'.

The people who sold me the house were a family of three, the parents about my age with another baby on the way. All I knew of the husband was that he was a hospital administrator and that he seemed impatient to sell.

'The vendor says he's had enough of the back-and-forth,' the estate agent told me on the phone after I'd asked for money off to fix a patch of rising damp in the corner of the living room. 'He says if you really want the property you must sign the contract within the week or he'll pull out.'

—

I met the wife just once, when she popped over to give me a forwarding address.

'Just in case we've forgotten to tell someone we've moved,' she said on the doorstep, handing me a scrap of paper with a handwritten address and phone number on it. 'We're only round the corner.'

She was a woman of unmemorable size with unmemorable hair and an unmemorable English accent, possibly southern counties. She wore unmemorable clothes and glasses and pushed an unmemorable baby in a pram. I'll never forget that day we met.

When I looked at the address, I was startled. The street was almost literally around the corner – about a five-minute walk away. Nick lived with his wife and two kids just a couple of roads down.

It struck me that those houses were slightly larger than mine, but not by much.

'What made you move so close?' I asked, trying not to sound suspicious.

'Oh, we just love Walthamstow and couldn't bear to leave the area,' she said, shaking a rattle at her baby. 'We wanted more space but all our money was tied up in the house, so we couldn't afford to make the renovations we wanted to.'

Then she said, 'I'm sad to leave this place, in a way. She's got real . . .' She looked up at the house. 'Character.'

She? I thought. I'd never heard anyone gender a house before, as if it were a boat. It seemed an odd thing to say, but I thought it best not to pry.

She shifted on her feet. She seemed to be lingering, as if there was something she wanted to ask me but couldn't decide how. 'So, how are you settling in? No issues, I hope?'

'None at all,' I lied. 'All fine.'

I don't know why I didn't bring up the burned floorboards. She had to have known about them – you could feel one or two of the holes with your feet through the carpet, which I know they must have laid because it wasn't in the pictures of the sales listing when they'd bought it in 2016. She eyed the house up and down again, nodded and flashed what might have been a smile. 'It took us a while to really feel at home here. But give it time and I think you'll really love it. Good luck!'

And with that, her smile opened out and she walked away in the direction of her new home. I never saw her again.

This was a week or so after Nick and I had found the burn patch which, for the time being, I covered with a very ugly faux-Persian IKEA rug that somebody had given me. I placed my bed on top of that. Still, lying there each night, my imagination burned.

The most troubling thing was that most fires, for obvious reasons, start in kitchens, not bedrooms. This one had obviously been significant, on the exact spot where a bed must once have been. Where my bed was now. My homebuyer's survey had mentioned nothing of a fire. And while the damage appeared to be only cosmetic, it didn't take a joiner to see the boards needed replacing. Had someone really fallen asleep with a lit cigarette in hand? Maybe a candle-lit seance gone wrong? Or perhaps an electric blanket *had* caught fire.

The thought of this thrust my mind back to a local horror story from my childhood. Near where we grew up in Islington, an elderly widow had died in her council flat after her old electric blanket burst into flames while she slept. Rumours were that she'd been too frail to even attempt escaping the house. It was said firefighters found her still curled up in bed, her body stiff and crisp. Even now, I'm reminded of that terrible image every time I read about a house fire in the news.

That night, as I lay in bed with Jasmine asleep next door, thoughts of what could have happened in my bedroom pinballed about my mind. In the darkness, I imagined smoke filling the house, pressing against the ceilings, seeping through keyholes and crevices. I could picture the flames licking up the walls, bursting through doorways, blistering paint.

What – or who – had started the fire? Was anyone in the house when it happened? The windows were the sort that only open at the top and aren't nearly wide enough to climb out. In this house, the only escape route was down the stairs and through the front door. Had anyone been trapped inside? Did someone burn to death where I now lay, like the old lady in Islington?

—

The next morning, my mind swirled with dark thoughts. So, I got Jasmine together, walked her to school and, as soon as I got home, fired up my laptop to look at old images of the house on Google Street View. As I clicked through the years – 2020, 2018, 2015 – nothing much changed: same uPVC porch, same uneven white facade, same windows, until . . . *There!* One image stood out above all others. I almost choked on my muesli.

The image was from June 2008, and showed the house as I knew it, except . . . where the windows should have been, there were corrugated iron sheets held in place by crooked wooden batons. Above the window frames, sooty marks curled up the front of the house like giant horror-clown eyelashes. The gutters were melted, mangled, and the facade's white-painted render was peeling as if ravaged by some flesh-eating disease.

A muddled anger rose inside me. How had the vendors not mentioned any fire? They surely knew about the burn patch in the bedroom as they themselves had laid the elephant-coloured carpet to cover it up. That said, it clearly wasn't in their interest to share that information if they could get away with it; I would only have demanded a discount to have it fixed. No, it was the surveyor who should've picked it up. Cowboys! I was cheesed off about that, but more with myself for scrimping on the survey. If there's one thing I dislike, it's an expensive lesson in how stingy I am.

As I calmed down, curiosity flared up. How serious had the fire been? Who was living in the house at the time? Was anyone hurt, or worse? Was it just the one fire, or had there been more? In my gut, something felt calamitously wrong. I had to know what happened to my house.

A trawl of the *Waltham Forest Echo* from the time shed no light. But there was another option: the London Fire Brigade. They would have records. And under the Freedom of Information Act rules, they would have to tell me, so long as: a) the request doesn't breach another person's privacy or the Official Secrets Act; b) is not too much of a faff for authorities to fulfil; and c) doesn't cost them more than £600 to process. It was worth a shot. As a reporter, I'd done this many times before. So I fired off an email.

Three weeks later, a response came in.

Dear Matt,

Thank you for your Freedom of Information request in relation to how many times the London Fire Brigade attended [the address] in Walthamstow, London.

In response, we have checked with our data team and have confirmed that we do not have a record of attending *[that address]*, between January 1, 2008 and January 1, 2016.

Kind regards,

Shelly*

This did not make sense. How could the fire brigade not have attended this address at any point in 2008? The photo on Google clearly showed a house ravaged by fire. So, I screen-grabbed the image and wrote back.

* In the interests of privacy and discretion, Shelly is a pseudonym.

From: Matt Blake
Sent: 1 Feb 2021, 13:06
To: LFB Information Access

Subject: RE: RE: FOI REQUEST

Dear Shelly, thank you for kindly replying to my request. I have
a question, however. Are you sure the LFB never attended
this property in 2008? Only, I attach a screengrab of an image
Google shot in June 2008 (taken from Google Street View) of
the property with clearly very significant fire damage to it.
And it seems pretty inconceivable to me that this fire was not
attended to by firefighters. For transparency, I am the current
owner of this property, although I was not back in 2008 and
I am trying to understand what happened to my home that
caused such damage.

Any advice you can give me would be much appreciated.

Shelly replied a week later with a list that included eight entries
including a couple of rescues from upstairs windows, three fires
and a false alarm. But, curiously, none were at my address. I replied
again.

From: Matt Blake
Sent: 7 Feb 2021, 15:15
To: LFB Information Access

Subject: RE: RE: RE: FOI REQUEST

Dear Shelly, thank you very much for your kind reply. This is
most strange, as neighbours have told me several fire crews
attended this fire in 2008. Is it likely that the call out might not
have been logged for any reason? Again, apologies to go on
about this, I appreciate you are probably quite busy. I hope you
can advise me a little further.

Two months went by. Then came Shelly's reply.

From: LFB Information Access
Sent: 2 April 2021, 16:26
To: Matt Blake

Subject: RE: RE: RE: RE: FOI REQUEST

Dear Matt,

I hope you are well. I am very sorry for my delayed response.

Our Data team have been working on this query for you since September. To give you a bit of background in relation to information recorded for incidents attended by the LFB: although we do have some limited information recorded from 2001, we only started to record more detailed information since November 2008.

The limited information held for incidents that occurred prior to November 2008 did not always include address fields that could be picked up in our incident report. So although I provided you with a report in September 2021, it did not pick up all the incidents that occurred between 2006 and 2008 (specifically where address fields were blank/null fields).

The Data team have now improved the address information on the report, so there should be less blank/null fields. Using the new report, below is a complete list of incidents that occurred on *[that street]* between 2001 and 2008.

I hope you find this new information of use, if you have any further queries please let me know.

And there it was in sans serif, 10-point, black and white.

Since 2000, firefighters had attended the street exactly twenty times, nearly a third of which were to one address: mine. Four 'malicious false alarms' and two 'primary fires'. Stranger still, five of those incidents (including both fires) had taken place within a seven-month period, between February and September 2008.

The fire brigade wouldn't tell me whether anyone had died, or been hurt, and the police would later refuse to help on the grounds that telling me anything would breach privacy laws. And again, not a crumb in the local paper. Rather than solve the Mystery of the Burned Floorboards, this new information only deepened it.

I went outside and looked up at the house. Under the grey April sky, it looked eerily as it did in the Google photo, only healed. Two doors down, Jackie – a tough but compassionate woman who teaches at a local school and has lived on the street for more than twenty years – was smoking on her front step.

'Oh yeah, we all used to call yours the Fire House,' she said when I asked if she remembered any of its previous occupants. 'I remember the guy who lived there. Odd bloke. Came to London from India, I heard. Was staying with a family who was renting it at the time.'

'Odd?' I asked.

She took a long drag on her cigarette. 'Well, for one thing, he liked his fire a bit too much.'

'Fire?' I queried.

'Yeah, he used to light fires inside that front bedroom then come out and sit on the wall opposite to wait for the fire brigade to arrive. Calm as you like. I don't know if he set them on purpose or by accident, but one fire was so bad we thought it was going to take our house down with it. I'll never forget that night. My boys were terrified.'

Jackie tapped ash into a flowerpot. 'Of course, he's in prison now,' she stage-whispered. 'He got done for raping all those poor women. Murdered the last one in the kids' playground up the street. You know, the one by the leisure centre? The papers had a name for him. What was it again?'

She clicked her fingers as if waiting for the name to appear through a puff of smoke. Then she turned and called through her open front door. 'Michael! What did they call the man who lived in the Fire House? The one they locked up last year.'

Without a beat, her partner Michael's voice drifted out of an upstairs window.

'The E17 Night Stalker!'

Chapter 3

THE KILLER WHO LIVED HERE, PART ONE

Spring, 2009. London is thawing out from a freezing winter, while the world's worst economic crisis since the Second World War is hotting up. Barack Obama has entered the White House. Gordon Brown just hosted the G20 Summit of world leaders in London, sparking mass protests in London's streets. Michael Jackson just announced his fateful *This Is It* comeback residency at London's O2 Arena. War is still raging in Afghanistan. Meanwhile, in Walthamstow, a stranger rapist prowls the streets at night, looking for prey.

—

Shortly before midnight on 23 March 2009, a fifty-nine-year-old woman leaves her cats at home to pop to the cashpoint at the Sainsbury's supermarket on Walthamstow High Street. A stroke victim with reduced mobility in her left arm, she knows her benefit payment is coming into her account at twelve o'clock, and she needs to top up her electricity meter and pay the rent by morning. It is a Monday night, so the streets are quiet.

After withdrawing the cash she needs, she heads towards the nearby Jet petrol station where she knows she can complete both errands at once. It is just a short walk, and a route she knows well; she's made it many times before.

This is where he sees her.

By 12.15 a.m., she is walking home again. She doesn't know it yet, but she is no longer alone. She doesn't see him, but CCTV does: a man somewhere in his late twenties or early thirties, about five-foot-eight in height, with short hair and 'coffee-coloured' skin. It is dark, and he keeps to the shadows, but what cameras do pick up is what he's wearing: a biker-style leather jacket with two distinctive white stripes down the arms.

She reaches her flat and goes up the stairs. She notices a man is behind her now. She tells him to leave her alone. But he does not. Instead, he follows her up to her front door, makes an obscene remark, and forces his way in. Once inside, he attacks her, repeatedly punching her in the face before raping her on her own bed. During her ordeal, she'll later tell police, he says things to her with an accent. Horrible things. He even tears off her jumper, and takes it with him when he leaves, perhaps as a keepsake. Moments later, the same man is captured again by CCTV walking away from the property, down towards St James Street, past the Coach & Horses pub on the corner, the Michael Franklin chemist and the Sun City tanning salon, under the railway bridge, past the Cash Converters, and away into the night.

In 2008/9, there were 13,093 reported rapes in England and Wales, according to Home Office records.[1] A sixth of those were in London.[2] Unsurprisingly, then, what happened tonight doesn't make much more than a 'nib' in the local paper – a short 'news in brief' article, typically a single paragraph, printed at the edge of a larger 'page lead'. Police put up a sign at the scene asking if anyone has seen anything and conduct door-to-door inquiries. But nothing comes up. The case is filed as an open investigation.

—

It is almost exactly a month later, on the night of 21 April 2009. At 11.50 p.m., a forty-six-year-old woman leaves the hostel where she lives to take a walk. She's been struggling to sleep and hopes the night air might help to clear her head. As the woman reaches South Grove, barely a stone's throw from the scene of last month's attack, she feels a tap on her shoulder. She turns around. It is a man of between five-foot-seven and five-foot-nine in height, in his early thirties, with thick cropped hair, a round face and a dark skin tone, as she will later tell police.

Then, with a noticeable accent, he asks her if she knows where to 'score' drugs. She says she does, but that it is a short bus ride away. That doesn't suit the man. He says he doesn't have enough money for a bus, but he is happy to go on foot if she doesn't mind showing him the way. She agrees.

The pair haven't walked far when the man suddenly pulls out a flick knife and forces her down an alleyway that runs alongside the pavement, between a brick wall and an area thick with bushes. A neighbour will later describe this alleyway in court as 'an absolutely disgusting place . . . frequented by tramps who sleep, urinate and defecate in'.

'I have never walked through [it],' the neighbour will say, 'but have seen and smelt enough of it over the years to know it was shameful.'

At that moment, the woman screams for her life – a howl that pierces the night and wakes at least one resident in the flats behind. A second scream might have alarmed neighbours enough to call the police. But, before she can draw another breath, the man punches her in the face. He punches her so hard that she 'sees stars', she will say. He then tells her to remove her clothes and get onto a soiled mattress that happens to be lying in the dirt nearby. It is this moment, she later tells a crowded courtroom, that scares her more than what is to come: she thinks now that she is going to die. He rapes her. When he has finished, he cleans himself with her underwear, throws it to the ground, and tells her to stay where she is. Then he walks off into the night.

—

Violent stranger rapes are rare enough. But two on the same stretch of road, each within a month of the other, can surely mean only one thing. Suffice to say, this rapist is no criminal mastermind; he has not been shy with his DNA. Only, when investigators run the two samples through the UK National DNA Database, neither draws a match.

They are hunting a ghost.

Eight days later, in the early hours of 29 April, police receive a call from a concerned resident of Markhouse Road. It is 2 a.m. and he says he has just been woken up by the sound of a woman screaming and moaning. It is coming from the churchyard of St Saviour's Church, next to his house. When officers arrive, they find a thirty-two-year-old woman lying in the bushes. She is semi-conscious, partially clothed, and it is clear she has been beaten and sexually assaulted. Her jaw is broken in multiple places, and she is suffering from a severe head injury. After treating her at the scene, a paramedic gently wraps her in a red London Ambulance Service blanket and takes her to hospital, where she spends the next month and a half recovering from her injuries, followed by a lengthy outpatient rehabilitation programme.

When detectives finally get the chance to interview the victim, she has no recollection of the attack whatsoever. She cannot even accept at first that she has been raped. All she remembers is popping out to the Cansin minimarket on Lea Bridge Road in the early hours. She recalls that, on the way, a man with 'bobbly' hair grabbed her arm and asked if she was okay. She told him she was fine and to leave her alone. But she noticed him again in the shop as she paid for her drink, an observation CCTV later confirms. The last thing she remembers is being followed by an Asian man as she passed the church. Nothing more.

DNA recovered from the red ambulance blanket matches that of both the previous attacks, which each took place barely 800 metres down the road from St Saviour's Church.

It is important to note that, under British law, victims of any kind of sex crime – from flashing to rape – have automatic anonymity for life, from the moment an offence has been reported. That means to even publish information that could lead to their identification by anybody is itself a crime. While their names and identities remain protected, these are real women with real lives that have been irrevocably damaged by these events. As a judge will later remark, they deserve more than to be 'reduced to anonymised letters or simply referred to as victims 1, 2 and 3'. Rather, they are individuals forced to 'live with the trauma [of what happened to them] for the rest of their lives'.

—

At the Met Police's North East Command Unit headquarters, a pattern appears to be emerging. But with no hard evidence as to the identity of Walthamstow's mystery rapist, detectives are stumped. It's time to go public. They put posters up at the 158 bus stop by the churchyard and in shop windows along Markhouse Road. Uniformed officers go door to door with CCTV stills and a photofit, asking residents if they have seen anything that could help identify the man in the black jacket. They even give out police-issue rape whistles to women in the area, telling them to be vigilant when out at night.

'I still have my whistle somewhere,' Angela Gold, a South African radiologist who lived in the area at the time, will tell me fifteen years later. 'Many women I knew were really scared. It really felt like evil was amongst us. I mean, from the locations of the attacks, it sounded like this guy lived around the corner. For all I knew I had sat next to him on a bus.'

Except, buses are not this man's primary hunting ground. That much is clear. He prefers supermarkets, shops or garages. Places that grow quiet at night. Places near where he lives that open out onto dark streets. They are the places he knows lone women will come. They are brightly lit with security cameras and staff; they feel safe. All he has to do is wait.

—

Michelle Samaraweera should feel safe on the five-minute walk from her boyfriend's home to the Somerfield supermarket on Markhouse Road. She's only popping out to buy snacks for a couple of friends who've come over for the evening. She tells them she won't be long as she puts on her black jacket and walks out the door. Michelle is, after all, a woman known for her boundless generosity who never hesitates to go out of her way to do nice things for the people she loves.

So, a little before one o'clock in the morning on 30 May 2009, the thirty-five-year-old widow leaves the house and walks alone down Queen's Road, in and out of the orange pools of light cast by street lamps along the way, until she comes out onto Markhouse Road. There, right ahead, is the Somerfield, illuminated by the all-night lights of the adjoining Texaco garage forecourt.

The day has been unseasonably cool, punctuated by sporadic showers. By now, the mercury has dropped to 8°C, and the air is heavy with moisture. The waxing crescent moon hangs limply over London, struggling to pierce the veil of scudding clouds. There are no bars or late-night takeaways along this stretch of road, so few have any reason to be out this late. Markhouse Road is quiet. A lone fox may have scurried out from under a parked car and across the road; a taxi may have trundled past. Somerfield is the only establishment open now. Inside, there are no customers, just a cashier on the graveyard shift.

At 1 a.m., the shop's CCTV picks up Michelle entering through the store's sliding doors. She's carrying her handbag, and wearing blue jeans, a white T-shirt and a dark jacket. Her shoulder-length black hair sweeps lightly across her face.

As she walks the aisles, she knocks over a can of Pringles, which she diligently picks up and puts back. She continues to peruse the shelves, picking out her groceries – some Cadbury's Cream Eggs, biscuits, a few packets of crisps.

Exactly six minutes after Michelle enters the empty store, a man comes in. He's wearing a leather jacket with two white stripes down the arms. Unlike Michelle, he is uninterested by what is on the shelves. Yet he walks with purpose from aisle to aisle, looking, listening, assessing. Then, a minute and a half later, he leaves without buying anything.

Meanwhile, Michelle pays the cashier £16 for her groceries and loads them into two branded 'bag for life' shopping bags. Then, twelve minutes after she first entered, the same camera captures Michelle leaving the shop. This is the last time Michelle Samaraweera is seen alive.

—

Nobody knows exactly what happened next. Nobody except the man in the leather jacket with the stripes. It is likely she crossed Markhouse Road and began to walk home along Queen's Road, opposite. She will have passed the Lighthouse Methodist Church on the left, which doubles as a polling station on election days, then Walthamstow Leisure Centre on the right, where locals play squash and children take gymnastics classes. She will have walked alongside the metal railings of the leisure centre car park before reaching a small astroturfed children's playground.

Here is where he likely intercepted her. We know there was a struggle because three neighbours in the houses opposite said they heard screaming that was 'consistent with someone being shut up'. But nobody came. We know she was raped, and we know she was strangled. We know she fought for her life. We also know that she died on the astroturf of that children's playground at the hands of a predator. Not just a predator, but also – as would become clear – a coward.

All of that happened sometime between 1:12 a.m. and 1.30 a.m. But it wasn't until 5.45 a.m. that a dog walker found Michelle's body, lying semi-clothed by the climbing frame. She had scratches on her face and blood on her hands, and her own hair under her nails – all this from trying to fight back, to somehow loosen whatever was around her neck. An arm from behind, maybe, or a 'soft ligature', as her autopsy would suggest. Beside her were her two shopping bags, still full. And beside them was a pool of blood.

Chapter 4

THE FOOTSTEPS OF EVIL

It was almost dark by the time I'd finished reading about the terrible things he did. I closed my laptop. I felt sick. The air in the living room seemed thicker, closer. The darkness outside pressed against the glass, as if trying to force its way in. I looked around the room. The dim light from the street lamps barely filtered through the curtains, casting long, distorted shadows across the piecemeal furniture I'd cobbled together. Over the years as a reporter, I've crossed paths with plenty of bastards: gangsters, hitmen, bent coppers, national newspaper editors. But this suddenly felt like the closest I'd come to real evil.

I tried to reason myself out of it. This must happen to homeowners all the time, I told myself. If there are 27 million homes in Britain, the chances of moving into a house with a dark past can't be that slim. Can it? I thought that if I could quantify my unease and reduce what I'd learned to a cold, hard number, maybe this wouldn't feel so lightning-strike unlucky. So lonely.

I reopened my laptop, and typed: *what are the chances of living in a house with a dark past?* Unsurprisingly, nobody has ever bothered to crunch the numbers. Even if the Office of National Statistics (ONS) were to try, there are too many variables to contend with. But that didn't mean I couldn't make some back-of-an-envelope calculations.

To start, you'd have to define 'dark past' – a nebulous enough term as it is. For the sake of argument, let's start with murders. According to the ONS, an average of 114 people were murdered at home per year between 2021 and 2024 – 70 per cent of them women.[1] That's roughly 11,400 domestic homicides across the last century. If we assume these are evenly distributed across the UK's 27 million homes[2] (a huge 'if', as we'll see), that translates to a 0.042 per cent probability that your home was the site of a homicide in the last hundred years.

So, there. In stark terms: you have about a 1 in 2,368 chance of living in a murder house in Britain.

But this figure forms only part of the picture. It doesn't, for example, account for age of the property or socioeconomic background. Murders are statistically more likely to occur in lower-income neighbourhoods, for instance,[3] while an old house, which most British homes are, is bound by time to absorb more lives, more shadows on its walls.

So actually, the chance of moving into a house where there's been a murder could be much higher than 1 in 2,368, depending on when and where it was built. That figure shrinks even further when you factor in suicides, tragic deaths, violence, abuse or even, like my house, the most subjective of all variables: the presence of evil.

—

The E17 Night Stalker committed no crimes inside my house itself, as far as I knew. Nobody died here, not at his hands at least.

And, if he did have anything to do with the fires, I have no reason to believe they were treated as arson. But it was where he came home; where he cleaned himself up, washed his clothes, scrubbed his fingernails. It's where he lay in bed and thought his thoughts. Where he dreamed, *if* he dreamed.

My thoughts were breeding fast. Did that third step creak for him as he crept up to bed, as it creaks for me? Did he feel the cool spot on the sixth step, or the draft by the back door when the wind picks up? Did he ever notice the strange pattern the moonlight makes on the bedroom wall as it shines in through the sycamore on cloudless nights? Did the front door key stick for him when he let himself out?

The house suddenly felt like an accomplice to unspeakable horror. My mouth was dry. I got up and walked to the kitchen to make a cup of tea. No milk. I'd have to pop to the shop. The nearest one was the Co-op attached to the petrol station, formerly a Somerfield. *The* Somerfield.

As I moved the house key towards the door I was struck by a cold realisation. I knew from the Google Street View images that this door hadn't changed since at least 2008. For all I knew, this could have been *his* key. Unlikely. But his would certainly have been identical. I turned it over in my hand, feeling the cool metal on my skin. I shuddered at the grim connection I now had with the man who might once have held it.

I still knew nothing about his circumstances. Nobody on the street seemed to know where the people with whom he lived had gone. Another neighbour from about eight doors down, Brian, told me he remembered a family living there but not their names. 'I saw them about, but they kept themselves to themselves,' he said.

'Renters, I think. They disappeared soon after the fires and I never saw them again. Can't have been habitable for a while though. Then . . . it just sat there, empty for years. The landlord didn't even bother fixing it up – left it with those sooty marks up the walls and twisted gutters. Wouldn't be surprised if he couldn't get rid of it. Though, there was something odd I noticed at the time . . . The curtains did occasionally change position, even though the place was supposed to be empty. Gave me the creeps.'

—

The door clicked behind me as I went out. I felt a light breeze wash over me and it smelled like rain. My shoulders loosened as I breathed in the fresh air. The noise of traffic in the distance, though muffled, carried a kind of reassurance, the sound of a world beyond the house's walls. It felt good to be outside.

Then something else hit me: I had to be retracing his footsteps on the night he killed Michelle Samaraweera. Past the same bay windows and bare trees; over the wonky paving stone at the bend in the road, through the same pools of lamplight. On reaching Markhouse Road, I came to the petrol station. Looming in the lilac sky, about 500 metres up, I could see the church spire in whose shadow he attacked his third victim. I turned towards the supermarket.

The doors slid open, and I looked up at the CCTV camera trained on the shop's entrance. This camera, or one in this exact spot, captured Michelle Samaraweera as she exited through those sliding doors that damp May night, thirteen years before.

Beneath the sterile hum of the fluorescent lights, among the lonely rows of packaged snacks and instant meals, I felt unspeakably sad for her. For the terror she must have felt in those final moments – one minute buying nibbles, the next fighting for her life in the dark. And for her family whom, as I would learn, this man would put through an ordeal of unfathomable depth, wilfully prolonging their pain for many years after he killed her.

As I paid for the milk, the cashier smiled from behind the Perspex security barrier and placed it in a carrier bag. I left the shop, back under the CCTV camera's gaze, and walked home. It was fully dark now. As I put the key back in the lock, I shuddered once more over this increasingly familiar routine: push key in lock, key sticks in lock, jiggle key in lock. Click.

—

At home, my mind had to squint when it peered into the dark little space where our lives intersected. And in squinting, the rest of the picture blurred. As the weeks slipped by, I grew increasingly obsessed with this house as the staging area for his depravity, as if it had become wrapped in the horror of what he did.

In public, I told people about the fires and the floorboards and the Google search and the fire brigade and the children's playground around the corner, and Michelle. It was a terrible story and people ate it up.

But privately, the story was turning parasitic. It became an unwanted squatter in my brain, claiming rights over my thoughts: about the lives he ruined, the connection we now had.

When I did tell the story to friends, I mostly glossed over the details of his crimes. The things he said to his victims during the attacks. The things he did to them. Those things were just too horrifying to say out loud, too grimly prurient.

Until I'd moved into my house, I'd always been cynical about the idea of lingering energy. But more than one of my friends, after hearing my story, told me with serious looks: 'I really think the sellers should have told you about this.'

'They had no obligation to tell you about this,' Sam Cook, partner at the British law firm Ellisons and a specialist in property litigation, told me. He reminded me that the starting point for any property negotiation is, and always has been, *caveat emptor* – Latin for 'let the buyer beware'. 'Ultimately, it is up to you as the buyer to satisfy yourself that the quality of the property is sound and isn't blighted in some way,' he said.

In Britain, there is legal precedent for this.[4] In 1998, Alan and Susan Sykes bought a three-bedroom detached home at 16 Stillwell Drive in Wakefield, West Yorkshire. Only, within weeks of moving in, they watched a Channel 5 documentary about the dental lecturer Samson Perera, who had murdered his step-daughter Nilanthie fourteen years prior, hiding her body parts about his home. That home, the Sykeses were shocked to discover, was *their* home.

The Sykeses instantly moved out, sold it at a loss of thousands of pounds and sued the former owners for failing to tell them about its gruesome past. The case went to the court of appeal, where a panel of judges ruled that the vendors, James and Alison Taylor-Rose, had not been dishonest when they answered 'no' to a questionnaire that asked: 'Is there any information which you think the buyer may have a right to know?'

'You couldn't get a more subjective question if you tried,' said Cook. '*You* may think you have a right to know about a murder in your house, but did the vendor?'

According to Cook, when it comes to, say, a historic murder, the vendor might genuinely believe that it's no longer something that a buyer has a right to know. They might think it's irrelevant, especially if it was a long time ago, the property has changed hands a few times or been renovated. It is, therefore, entirely down to their interpretation of that question.

'The only way to protect yourself, if a dark past is something you're worried about, is to make your own bespoke inquiry about it,' Cook added. 'But remember, it is incumbent on the litigator to prove that the seller gave an incorrect representation.'

To put it another way: you will have to prove that the vendor knew about the dark past and then lied about it.

When it comes to ghosts, the legal position is even flimsier. 'Does a buyer have a legal right to know that a property is haunted?' wondered Cook. 'Well, even if it is a famously haunted property, a vendor could simply say, "Ghosts aren't real so why would I mention it?"'

Cook chuckled. 'It's not a case I can see any court taking seriously.'

The only way to protect yourself, then, is to do the research yourself. The trouble is, on top of a mortgage application, survey acquisition and solicitor's searches, that could turn into a hell of a lot of work. You'd have to delve into local archives, historical societies, and potentially even track down ex-residents to piece together the property's history. If only there were a service that could do it all for you . . .

Well, in America there is. It's called DiedInHouse.com – a 'death directory' that can tell potential homebuyers about the past of any US property. It is the brainchild of US landlord and software entrepreneur Roy Condrey, who launched the service in 2013 after noticing a gaping hole in the market. I wanted to know how he could have helped me. So, I called him up.

'If there's a fire or if you've had repairs, you have to disclose that by law,' Condrey told me. 'Why not a death? Especially a violent death.'

For a fee, DiedInHouse will trawl through more than 130 million police and court records, news reports, obituaries, death certificates and credit histories. For belt and braces, his team then performs a manual search to 'try to fill any holes the algorithm might have missed'. And the algorithm won't just look for violent deaths, but violent crimes, break-ins, thefts, former 'hoarder houses', fires, murder-suicides, accidental deaths, ex-funeral homes and gang-related activities.

Business is booming. Condrey said he has sold hundreds of thousands of reports since he started – an average of around 100 a day. 'No matter what people say, murder impacts a lot of people. I know it does,' he said. 'If people didn't care, they wouldn't be buying our reports.'

For an idea of how it works, consider the White House. A future US president might like to know that thirteen people have died there since it was built in 1792, according to its DiedInHouse report. They include two sitting presidents, three First Ladies, a White House press secretary, three children, and a drunk truck driver who crashed a stolen plane onto the South Lawn in 1994.

As a point of order, American patriots may be relieved to know that the White House has never been a meth lab, nor has it – at the time of writing – ever housed a registered sex offender. As a second point of order: this does not include presidents found guilty of sexual abuse in civil courts.

'Interestingly, we've observed that individuals who initially claim indifference often change their stance when confronted with specific information,' Roy told me. 'Whether it's the fear of dark energy, concerns about feng shui, the allure of morbid tourism, or the implications for resale value, people want to be informed.'

DiedInHouse has done so well in the USA that Condrey wants to expand the service into Britain. But there is one snag. 'Our algorithm mainly works on digitised records, most of which only go back as far as the eighties,' he said. 'To go back further, we have to research a property manually. And in the UK, history goes back forever. You've got houses that are older than my country.'

Chapter 5

HECTOR AND
THE HAUNTED WOOD

That May, Louis, an old school friend, popped round for a belated housewarming pizza and drink. Louis is a top London chef with an easy laugh who is always first to the bar to buy beer for his friends. He's also the sort of person who would tell you straight if you had food in your teeth, if your joke isn't funny or, well, if your home had a weird vibe.

'Not being funny, Matt, but there's something not quite right about this place,' he announced almost as soon as he had walked through the door.

'What do you mean by that?'

'Sorry. No. I mean . . . I know you've just moved in, and maybe it's just because you haven't really put your stamp on it yet,' he backtracked, 'but I just . . . I don't know, I can't put my finger on it. The atmosphere feels . . . kind of heavy.'

A shadow must have passed over my face because then he said, 'No. Sorry. It's probably just me. Maybe it's because you told me about the burned floorboards. And the stairs are all the way over there, and that damp patch under the window, which I can smell. I'm sure it'll feel great when you've got all your stuff in.'

'This *is* all my stuff.'

He shifted guiltily. 'Oh. Look, mate. Forget I said anything. Sorry. I've put my foot in it, haven't I? Sorry, Matt. It's a nice place. Really!'

I wasn't cross with Louis. I was disappointed that he hadn't spotted something wonderful in the house that I hadn't yet found. He's one of the few friends I have with a spiritual side and, on some level, I wanted him to tell me my house was a magical space of dreams and harmony, the sort of place where rainbows begin.

But there's something else to know about Louis, as far as this story is concerned: he has a poltergeist at home whom he calls Hector.

'I was making dinner just last week and a bowl of cheese flew out of my hand and smashed against the wall,' he told me after the pizzas arrived. 'I didn't just drop it. It was Hector. He does stuff like that all the time. Once I came home from work to find the radio blasting out classical music. I know it wasn't on when I left that morning, and nobody had been home since. I can't tell you why or how it happened, but it did. It really freaked me out.'

I told him the same thing had happened to me, here. He nodded sagely. 'I know you're cynical about this stuff, but I'm telling you, weird shit happens in the world and it doesn't always have a rational explanation.'

Louis first encountered Hector after he and his wife, Sammy, visited a 500-year-old tumbledown cottage in the country. They were considering buying it cheap and doing it up. 'The builders were in there making it safe,' he said, 'and I picked up this little chunk of oak that had fallen off a beam. It was moving to think that I was touching something another human had made with their hands over half a century ago. I put it in my pocket and forgot about it.'

It wasn't until they returned to their flat that he remembered the ancient piece of wood and pulled it out. 'Sammy was angry with me for bringing it home,' he said. 'She thought I should have left it in that house, where it belonged.'

That's when the strange things began to happen: the radio blaring to life, mugs knocked out of hands, flickering lights. 'We believe he came with us in the wood,' Louis said. 'Nothing had ever happened before that piece of wood came into our home.'

'Why didn't you just throw it away?' I asked.

His face contorted. 'Throw it away? No way, wouldn't dare. No, no. Hector stays at home with us, where we can keep an eye on him.'

Louis doesn't believe in ghosts. Well, he doesn't believe Hector is the unquiet spirit of a dead peasant from the reign of Henry VIII. 'Those kinds of ghosts don't make sense to me,' he said. 'There are too many people on Earth and through history. It seems unfair that only some of them get to come back and haunt the living.'

We both laughed. 'But I do think that spaces retain energy,' he continued. 'The older the place is, the more stories it's got to tell, the more layers of the past that sit inside the walls. I can't tell you why I get a certain feeling about some places and not about others. But I have walked into buildings that didn't feel right. Definitely.'

'Like this place?'

'Sorry,' he said again.

'So, why do you call your poltergeist Hector, then?'

'I think it just helps to give it a name,' he said. 'Takes away his power to scare us and helps me make sense of something I fundamentally cannot understand.'

Louis smiled playfully. 'He's harmless, really. I sometimes just think he gets lonely and does things for attention.'

—

I have met many smart, sensible people who say they have seen ghosts. I know even more, like Louis, who believe in unseen energy that can dial into mood and perception or manipulate objects and communicate with the living.

Six months ago, I would have laughed mockingly in Louis's face. But since my phantom-radio event, I admit, my sceptical foundations were crumbling. Could Louis have a point? Could it be that my house was simply haunted by some sort of lingering energetic whisper from the past? Or – dare I say it – a ghost?

Einstein famously said energy cannot be created or destroyed; it can only change from one form to another. It has become a cliché rubbed smooth by paranormal enthusiasts who feel religion doesn't go far enough (even though Einstein himself never believed in ghosts). Some argue that all the electricity in our bodies, the stuff that makes our hearts beat and brains pulse, all the energy that powers us . . . it has to go *somewhere* after we die – it can't just evaporate into the air and the earth. *Can it?* Perhaps certain particles that 'make' us are held together by some hitherto undiscovered quantum force when our flesh decays? Is that what the religious call 'souls' – leftover fragments of ex-human energy coalescing on an alternative astral realm just beyond our blunt perception?

We must assume, with straight faces, that consciousness survives death and lives on within these cocktails of biological charge. Because, like the people they once were, ghosts differ in form and personality. Some are stuck to locations of deep personal meaning; others cling to the living. Some hang back to help loved ones, others to seek vengeance, and others remain simply because they're trapped between worlds. Their manifestations are just as diverse as their intentions; they appear as breaths, bangs, shadows, mists, orbs, chills, hushed voices, scents or full-body apparitions. If these 'ghosts' possess enough energy, they can even interact with the physical world by moving objects, leaving signals and – in extreme cases – manipulating people's emotions.

Is *that* what this was, then? I had simply moved into a haunted house. Perhaps the radio had been switched on by the unquenched spirit of a dead Britpopper fastened to this place by unfinished business – an old Pulp fan needing to hear Jarvis Cocker's voice one last time before surrendering to the light.

Spell it out and it sounds far-fetched. But reports of such events outdate recorded history, crossing continents and cultures – a Babylonian tablet from 1500 BCE describing an exorcism is the earliest known depiction of a ghost.[1] Even today, while we live in an increasingly secular environment, belief in the supernatural is growing. YouGov has found that British people are significantly more likely to believe in ghosts (34 per cent) than in a creator (27 per cent).[2] In another survey, the polling agency revealed that 39 per cent of British people think a house can be haunted, 25 per cent have felt the presence of a supernatural being and 9 per cent have communicated with the dead.[3]

It's even more common in America, where 65 per cent of the

population 'believe in spirits or unseen spiritual forces', according to the Pew Research Center,[4] while 81 per cent of adults say 'there is something spiritual beyond the natural world, even if we cannot see it'. Far fewer (17 per cent) believe 'the natural world is all there is'.

The reasons for this growth are complicated and difficult to pin down.

Camera phones play a big part. Never in history have people recorded so many ghostly encounters, nor shared them on such an industrial scale. Unsurprisingly, sociologists at the University of Delaware found in 2024 that increased use of video-led social platforms such as TikTok and YouTube leads to stronger belief in the paranormal.[5] Social media, in other words, has become an open-invite campfire circle for the digital age, only instead of uplighting faces with the glow of a torch, now it's the cold, white glare of a smartphone.

So, whether I believe in the supernatural or not, the fact remains that a vast portion of the world does. And that belief shapes actions, decisions, lives. I once met a man who continued to catch the scent of his father's leather jacket for years after he committed suicide – in the supermarket, the cinema, 'the most random of places'. 'It gives me comfort to know he's not just vanished into nothing,' he told me. Another friend and staunch rationalist, persuaded to visit a medium after the death of her grandfather, later said to me, 'I was telling myself throughout the consultation that it was all just clever sleight of mind, but she knew things about my granddad that she couldn't possibly have known. Personal, specific, secret things. It honestly felt like my granddad was in the room with us. It really shook me up.'

Believing in the supernatural doesn't make you stupid. Its proponents include some of history's sharpest minds. Winston Churchill claimed to have been confronted by the ghost of Abraham Lincoln at the White House, as he stepped naked out of the bath. 'Good evening, Mr President,' he told the bearded spectre. 'You seem to have me at a disadvantage.'[6]

Arthur Conan Doyle – creator of literature's most famous rationalist, Sherlock Holmes – spoke to ghosts through mediums (the British Library holds a recording of his own alleged spirit speaking from beyond the grave),[7] while Alan Turing, the computer scientist, believed in telepathy.[8] Then there is the psychoanalyst Carl Jung, who explored concepts like synchronicity, which he described as meaningful coincidences that could not be explained by chance, and had a lifelong interest in the paranormal.[9] Even the evolutionary biologist Richard Dawkins, Britain's God-denier-in-chief, told an auditorium in 2018, 'I confess that I would hesitate to stay in a notoriously haunted house'.[10]

As our bodies metabolised pizza into energy that may one day power our own ghosts, Louis and I circled back to the subject of my house. I showed him the burned floorboards and told him about Vyas, and he breathed it all in with an open mouth.

'So, what are you going to do?' he said. 'Are you going to sell it? You can't stay here now, surely.'

The anxiety I had gone through to find somewhere to live was still raw. And the idea of having to go through it all again, of putting Jasmine through another move; of dealing with more estate agents, mortgage brokers, building surveyors, impatient sellers, sharp-elbowed viewings . . . it filled me with a pulsating dread.

'I don't know,' I said. 'I've only been here five months. Any new buyer would want to know why I was selling up so quickly. What would I say?'

Louis shook his head. 'If it were me, I'd be straight onto Rightmove – I wouldn't live there another night. Not after . . .' He shuddered. 'I honestly don't know how you can stay here knowing what you now know.'

Louis buttoned up his coat and shook off a shiver. 'Think about it. We leave traces of ourselves everywhere – fingerprints, hair, even our DNA. But what about our energy? Our emotions? The things we do in a place, the experiences we have . . . That's got to leave some kind of imprint, right?'

I was sceptical. 'It's been more than a decade since he lived there. So even if he did leave an energy, I can't believe it could still be there now.'

He shrugged. 'Believe what you want but I just don't think I could be happy in a house with a past like that. The thought gives me the creeps for you. What if some of his evil matter has been clinging to the walls and floors all these years?'

He took a deep breath. 'And what if, while you're there . . . What if . . . it starts to seep out?'

Chapter 6

THE PHANTOM DOORBELL

It happened in the dead hour. 3:34 a.m. A Sunday. The night was draped in a silence so profound that even the wind had forgotten to rustle the sycamore's leaves outside. It was one of those evenings when the world – certainly Walthamstow – seemed to hold its breath. Although I hadn't been sleeping well since learning of the house's past, that night I'd sunk into a corpse-like slumber. No dreams, just pillow dribble. Mine, Jody's and Jasmine's breathing was the only sign of life in the otherwise still house.

Jody jolted upright, clutching the covers. She touched my arm.

'Did you hear that?' she whispered, wide-eyed. My sleep-addled mind grappled to catch up.

'Hear what?' I mumbled, reaching groggily for the bedside lamp.

'The doorbell,' she said, her voice a thin thread. 'Someone rang it.' The idea seemed absurd. Who would be at the door at 3:34 a.m.? Still, a prickle of unease danced down my back.

'Must have been a dream,' I offered and rolled over, not wanting her to see my open eyes as I listened through the darkness.

In the five months I'd known her, Jody had always been level-headed, not prone to flights of fancy. Her cool, sceptical confidence was one of the things that had attracted me to her in the first place. 'No,' she said sharply, 'I heard it clearly. It *was* the doorbell.'

—

Jody had bought me this doorbell as a gift the previous month.

'I don't need a bell,' I said. 'People can just knock.'

'Yes, you do. You need to know when someone's at the door, and you can't hear a knock from upstairs in this house. What if someone important comes to the door?'

'Like who?' I said. 'I don't know anyone important.'

'Aren't *I* important?' she laughed, then she clapped her hands and pointed at me with a satisfied grin. 'What about the Amazon delivery driver? Or Deliveroo! Or the police to arrest you for wearing that terrible white fluffy hoodie you refuse to throw away.'

She was talking about what Jasmine had started calling my 'polar bear hoodie' which I'd bought to keep me warm in the winter in the vain hope it'd help me save money on heating bills. It hadn't.

Jody made a fair point. So, I begrudgingly stuck the button part to the doorframe outside the house and plugged the receiver into a socket in the kitchen. The moment it got a taste of electricity it let out a deafening electric chime, like an asthmatic chipmunk with a trumpet.

'You're welcome,' Jody called down from upstairs.

That month the bell did its job with gusto. The police never came, but Amazon and Deliveroo both gave it a good workout.

My relationship with Jody had been going well and she had been spending a lot more time with me at the house. So well, in fact, that she'd started ordering her own Amazon deliveries to my address after parcels started going missing in the lobby of her own apartment building in Hackney. In other words, when the bell went off in the middle of the night, she knew what she had heard.

—

'Go and see who's at the door,' she said impatiently.

Sighing, I shuffled groggily down the stairs. The house felt uncomfortably quiet. I flicked on the hallway light and opened the front door. The glow from inside spilled out onto an empty, breezeless street. Not even a cat in sight.

My mind was swarming. There was no sign of a power cut, which would have set the bell off as it did that first day I plugged it in. The streetlights were on, and the oven clock would be flashing 00:00 if the power had gone out. But it told the correct time: 03:43.

Standing in the kitchen, I stared at the doorbell receiver plugged into the socket. Its little green light blinked innocently. A surge of irritation flared. A malfunction, then. These things happen, even with new technology.

'Anything?' Jody called out.

'Nothing,' I snapped, more harshly than I'd intended. I still felt slightly wobbled. 'Probably just a glitch. Go back to sleep.'

—

The next morning, I made my way downstairs and opened the front door. The world outside continued as normal. A van emblazoned with the words 'loft-conversion specialist' trundled past. A power tool screeched. A dog walker whistled a cheerful tune, twirling a bag of dog shit like a bunch of keys. Yet, I couldn't shake the nagging tremor of the night before.

'Morning,' Jody greeted me, the hint of a question mark in her voice as she studied me over her coffee mug.

'Morning,' I replied, unable to look her in the eye. The doorbell . . . It was real. It had surely happened. Jody couldn't have been mistaken . . . could she? Her words bounced between my ears. *I heard it clearly . . .*

Perhaps it was lack of sleep, but a headache was beginning to mushroom inside my skull as the weight of it all pressed down on me. I poured myself a cup of coffee and slurped it. Its bitter taste felt oddly cathartic.

'Maybe it was a power surge,' I said. But even as I said it, I knew it wasn't true. The oven clock was proof of that.

Jody shrugged, her pragmatic nature reasserting itself. 'Could be a glitch in the system. A faulty product. These things happen.'

I lifted the coffee cup to my lips too quickly and the liquid sloshed over the rim, onto my polar bear hoodie. I stared at the spreading brown stain, a sickly feeling washing over me.

'It's nothing,' I insisted, thinly.

Jody reached across the table, squeezing my hand. 'Hey, don't worry about it,' she said. 'It's probably nothing.'

Her touch was warm, grounding. I wanted to believe her, to let go of the unease that had settled in the pit of my stomach. But the doorbell . . . it had happened. And the knowledge of the house's past, of the terrible man who lived here, loomed over my mind. I remembered what Louis had said about energy.

'I know,' I said, forcing a smile. 'It's just . . . something Louis said the other day. This house. It's got a lot of history.'

Jody nodded. She seemed to understand. 'Well, you're making new history now, you and Jasmine,' she said.

'I guess so,' I said. 'Probably just a glitch.'

—

The mice moved in that spring. Maybe they were here all along. Or maybe building work along the street had flushed them my way. 'These old houses, they've been knocked about so much over the years, they're like mouse highways,' one of my elderly neighbours had grumbled when I asked if mice were a 'thing' on the street. 'Nothing you can do.'

But as the days got warmer, the mice grew bolder. As is always the way with mice, it's the droppings you notice first – little clusters of black pellets the size of rice grains. Initially I found them in the kitchen drawer where I keep pots and pans, then under the dishwasher, and along the skirting boards. It was an IKEA kitchen installed by the previous owners. The drawer beneath the sink, which held two small bins for rubbish and recycling, had no back panel. Just a bare wall with a hole for the sink's wastepipe to escape, and a half-inch gap between the back of the cupboard and the wall. I found my first mouse there, nibbling a small crust of toast that must've fallen down the side of the bin.

There followed my first game of, well, Matt and mouse – a half-hour battle of wits that always went the same way: I'd corner it in a cupboard or behind the fridge, where it would crouch, terrified, staring and twitching when I moved in as if to bludgeon it with the broomstick handle. Every time I came in for the kill, it dashed to another corner of the kitchen until, eventually, it made a successful bid for freedom behind the kitchen sink.

The mouse hadn't come alone. Soon, its brothers and sisters had migrated into the living room. More than once, while I was watching television at night, one would run out from under the sofa, between my legs, and freeze in the middle of the rug. We'd look at each other, stock still, waiting to see who would make the first move. It was always me, and the mouse would always escape.

But it seemed that the mice were most keen on that spot beneath the bins, where crumbs fell from scraped plates, and they would gather there to nibble at the constant spill. I put the broomstick against the wall, ready to unleash on their heads. But they were always too fast for me. Traps didn't work either. I put them everywhere – behind the bins, along the walls, back of cupboards. I learned from YouTube that the best bait is a dollop of peanut butter or piece of breakfast cereal superglued to the pressure pad. Only, each morning when I checked the traps, instead of the corpse of a greedy mouse, I'd find the bait nibbled or licked around its edges into a delicate cone. In the end, I came late in life to the fundamental truth: If you want a job done properly, pay a professional to do it for you.

The mouse-catcher did a full 'audit' of the house, plugging every hole and cranny with wire wool and expanding foam. He scorned my traps, threw them all away and laid poison stations in their place. 'You need a licence for this poison,' he told me in a meaty Latvian accent. 'It stops the rodent's ability to absorb water so they leave the house in search of a drink and die outside.' Then he frowned. 'It's not a nice thing, but rodents carry disease and poison is the only way to really get rid of them.'

Next came the slime.

No sooner than the mice had deserted, I came into the living room one morning to find a silky circle of slime across the hearth of the fireplace. It glinted in the light, all pastel pinks, yellows and blues. It was strangely beautiful. At first, I thought Jasmine must have gone rogue with a tube of Pritt Stick. But it wasn't sticky to the touch. Baffled, I followed the trail up the side of the fireplace, around my Sonos speaker, over the radio, up the wall and across the wall-mounted mirror. Too high for Jasmine, I thought. Then, near the ceiling, the trail stopped. It was as if whatever had made it had vanished on the spot.

The mystery was solved the following Saturday night while Jody and I watched TV. Ant and Dec had just come on and, as I lifted the remote to change channels, we heard a thud. Jody yelped and leaped from her seat.

'What the fuck was that?' she said, scouring the floor. 'Matt, it's a giant slug. What the hell is going on? It's literally raining slugs in your house.'

She wasn't wrong. Inches from where her foot had been, a slug lay stone dead. Or out cold. It was big for a slug – about the size and texture of a Mutant Ninja Turtle's thumb, or some other similarly proportioned appendage. I looked up. On the ceiling, another was slithering its way to nowhere. Then I noticed an even bigger one on the floor inching its way out from under the sofa.

Jody was already Googling 'slug infestations' on her phone, and I was again wondering how many slugs make an omen. 'Pretty sure when it starts to rain slugs you should call a priest,' I joked. She didn't laugh.

There had been slugs in the house since the first day I moved in. But that was before I'd furnished the place. Somewhere in my subconscious, I suppose, I assumed they'd gone away after realising the place was occupied again. But now I looked at the ceiling and I could see, from certain angles, pattern after pattern of slime circles, covering the surface like giant, glistening spirograph drawings.

Over the next few weeks, it got worse. They seemed to be growing braver, only ever coming out at night in droves. I know this because, most mornings when I came down for breakfast, I'd find fresh trails of silvery goo across my things. Every time I wiped them away, new ones appeared the next day. It was like an ethereal dirty protest, marking their territory with limacine secretion.

I could not understand how they were getting in. I thought I'd blocked all the holes after Mousegate. But still, they came. Slugs have always repulsed me on a primal level. Their bodies are too slimy, soft and alien to reasonably exist on dry land. They move with a silent, relentless purpose, like they're not just invading your space, they're violating it. Homeless snails coming for *my* shell! Their growing presence felt like a manifestation of what was going on inside my mind. Another sign that something was deeply wrong.

⸺

'Yes, I remember the fires in your house,' said Brenda, an elderly neighbour from further down the street. Brenda had lived in the same house for decades and was watering her window pots when I passed by. Nobody knew street business better than Brenda. 'Yes, yes, I vaguely remember the family who lived there. Asian. A man did live there. Wasn't there long. I heard people say he was a murderer. The night hunter, or something.'

She tipped the last few drips in her watering can onto a pot of geraniums. Then she said, 'But your house used to be famous on this street. There were the fires, we all remember those. Awful business. And after that, it was a farm for . . . you know . . .'

She raised her eyebrows, as if to say, *I don't need to say it out loud, do I?*

'A farm?' I said.

'Yes, you know. A grow house.'

At that moment, Ken, from the far end of the street, walked past. 'Morning, Ken,' said Brenda. 'I was just telling Matt how they used to grow cannabis in his house.'

'Ha, yes, that's right,' Ken grinned. 'It was around the time of the London Olympics. An Asian operation, maybe Chinese or Vietnamese.'

I buffered. 'Are you positive it was my house?'

Ken laughed again. 'Yes, it was definitely yours. I remember because it was a freezing winter, and your house was the only one on the street where snow never settled on the roof. You know, because of the hydroponic lights.'

—

It sometimes felt as if snow was settling *inside* the house. It got so cold. I noticed that some rooms in particular were distinctly colder than others, no matter how high I cranked up the heating. And there were specific spots that always felt chilly. One was on the stairs, about five steps up, just after the creaky board. I went through a phase, when I was alone, of stepping in and out of it on my way up to bed – warm, cool, warm, cool. There was no draft beneath the stairs. I could not work it out.

This was not the case in the 'Fire Room', where I slept. It was the warmest room in the house. Weirdly warm. Meanwhile, the living room was never anything but freezing. Bleeding the radiators made no difference. I began to spend more and more time in bed.

I'd lie under the covers, above the burned floor where fire twice raged, listening to the soft ticking of the clock on my wall – another remnant of the divorce. My thoughts invariably turned to the mess I'd made of my life.

The divorce had left a void in me, a hollow space that echoed with memories and regrets. I had hoped the move would fill that void, but as the days grew longer, the emptiness seemed to expand. I didn't exactly miss my ex-wife, and my relationship with Jody was going well. But I couldn't help but feel a profound sense of loss for the family I no longer had.

I was sadder than I knew how to admit. Not for the death of our marriage, but how it was affecting our daughter.

'Daddy,' Jasmine said one bedtime, squeezing Bunny. 'When I'm a baby again, will you and Mummy live together, like you did when I was a baby before?'

My heart froze. It turns out, explaining to a four-year-old how time runs inexorably in one direction is as impossible as explaining why two grown-ups can no longer share a home, let alone a bed. Desperately, I regurgitated some cliché about how lucky she was to have two homes. She just looked up at me with sad eyes.

'But I don't want two homes. I want one home.'

—

Lying in bed that night, I realised what every child of divorce already knows: the real monster under the bed is not the big bad wolf; it's abandonment. She began having recurring nightmares. In one, she said, her mother and I would sail away on a boat, leaving her alone in a forest. In another, we were all running from a tiger, only she couldn't keep up, and her mother and I wouldn't slow down. 'Then it caught me and bited me on my finger,' she explained.

I didn't know how to tell her that she'd be alright, that life is chaos and all things pass. I wasn't yet sure if I believed it myself. So that spring, I painted a giant rainbow on her bedroom ceiling. I bought a picture book called *Two Homes*, about an androgynous child called Alex who lives between her divorced mother and father's houses. Within a few months, we each knew every word by heart. It seemed to comfort her to know she wasn't the only child on Earth with two toothbrushes.

Something was happening to me too. Living alone, the pressures of single-parenthood. Add to that the mice, the slugs, the cold patches, the phantom doorbell and late-night radio . . . I told myself it must all have a rational explanation. Of course it did; aren't all these things simply the pitfalls of living in old houses?

But somewhere, deep down, a jagged sense of unease was taking root. Like the mice I was hunting, I began to skitter and jump at every creak and groan of the house. My nerves were fraying like old wiring. Sometimes, when I was alone, I thought I saw shadows move out of the corner of my eye, figures at the window. I found myself peering into dark recesses at night or holding my breath before turning on a bathroom light for fear of what might be standing behind me in the mirror. I had become a thirty-eight-year-old who was afraid of the fucking dark.

Logic told me it was just the stress, the accumulated weight of massive change. The divorce papers, the meals for one, the empty spaces where a wife used to be, the unbearable silence that filled the house when Jasmine was at her mother's. I tried to breathe new life into the place. To make it ours. I painted the living room in what I thought would be dusky pink but, on the wall, looked more the colour of a smacked arse. I hung bright yellow curtains and borrowed Jody's old sofa bed to hide the emptiness of this house. And yet, the more I put in, the emptier it felt – like pouring water into a bath with no plug. No matter what I did, it didn't feel as if the house belonged to us. It was, I was beginning to feel, like we belonged to it.

And soon, a new thought crawled in: was I just unhappy in this house? Or was the house *making* me unhappy?

Chapter 7

THE KILLER WHO LIVED HERE, PART TWO

The morning of 31 May 2009 began as mornings often did at The East Area Murder Command headquarters in East London. The coffee machine was putting in a shift as officers sifted through paperwork, held briefings and looked for new leads on open cases. Then, sometime after 6 a.m., the call came in. A woman's body had been found in a children's playground in Walthamstow. There was no question: it was murder.

Detective Sergeant Steve Lynch was new to the murder beat, having joined the division only the previous February. When news of Michelle Samaraweera's murder broke, as when news of any big job breaks, the building burst into a fever of 'organised chaos'.

'It's what we call a Category A job, the most serious job there is,' Steve told me. 'It's very rare that a job that serious comes in, and when it does, you might as well write the next two weeks off.'

Everyone knew what that meant: sleeping at desks, late nights, early mornings, all fuelled by a strict diet of coffee and takeaway food. 'If you've not got them within those first two weeks,' he added, 'then you're normally in it for the long haul.'

When I began to write this book, I asked the Metropolitan Police to help me gain a deeper insight into the investigation. But they refused on the baffling grounds that they don't help journalists writing books, only those writing articles for newspapers and magazines. 'In any event,' a press officer told me, 'a quick search suggests none of [the key officers involved] appear to be in the Met any longer.'

I tracked down Steve through a source, and he said he'd gladly talk to me so long as I didn't reveal anything about his life outside the force, including his current job. For a man who has spent a career putting some of London's nastiest criminals behind bars, this made sense. So, we met in a Costa Coffee by St James Street station on a warm summer's day in 2024. His order, unsurprisingly, was a large coffee, no milk, no sugar – he gave the distinct impression of a man who has put away a lot of strong coffee in his time.

Steve, who by the looks of him could have been anywhere between forty-five and fifty-five, retired from police service in 2019. He arrived in shorts and a golfing T-shirt, with neat grey hair and the tan of a man who's got retirement well figured out. Across a thirty-year career, his detective work spans from burglary to violent crime, celebrity crime to drug trafficking. He spent the last decade of his career as a detective sergeant in the 'murder squad'. It was there that, in 2010, he joined 'one of the most complex investigations the command has ever encountered'.

For the first few days after Michelle's murder, every available officer from the force's Homicide Command was drafted in to help. Steve was one of them. 'The Murder Command at that time consisted of about eight teams, each with thirty or so officers, so anyone who could be spared came aboard,' said Steve. 'We were then divided up and delegated tasks. One team took on the DNA profiling operation, another trawled through CCTV, another explored possible linked offences, and so on.'

Steve was assigned to house-to-house inquiries, visiting every home on every street within a 3.4-mile perimeter of the playground.[1] By the end, they'd knocked on more than 9,000 doors. Of course, the fantasy was that *he* would be standing behind one of those doors, that he would simply step out, offer his wrists and confess to it all. And if not him, then perhaps someone else would know something, have seen or heard something. Anything to give police a nudge in the direction of justice.

But, what if he did answer the door? Would the officer even recognise his face? It wasn't fully visible on the CCTV, though he hadn't been careful to hide it. So, on 12 June, the decision was made to launch a voluntary DNA sweep of men in the area who fitted the killer's description.[2] Soon, they'd recorded samples of around 1,100 volunteers in the area. 'It was a huge undertaking,' recalled Steve. 'I'm not sure if such a large DNA profiling operation had ever been done.'

And yet, somehow, the killer slipped through the net.

The local press had already begun piecing together a story. 'Warning to women over suspected serial rapist,' ran a headline of the *Waltham Forest Guardian* on 9 June 2009.[3] 'Killer "may have raped two more"', ran another.[4]

They had even come up with a nickname: the Calendar Killer, so called because of his tendency to strike at the end of each month. Local businesses started offering female employees taxi rides home and pubs put up signs to warn people to be on their guard late at night. That two-week golden window soon expired. Investigators were running out of options. So they turned to the press for help.

On 29 June, exactly a month after Michelle's murder, chief investigating officer Detective Inspector Stewart Hill appeared on BBC's *Crimewatch* alongside Michelle's elder sister Ann.[5] 'The nickname "the Calendar Killer" is misleading,' said DI Hill. 'This is an incredibly dangerous person. He could strike at any time.'

Then he added: 'It's possible that he's nocturnal. He may live close to the area and may be able to leave home without raising any suspicion from family or friends.'

While her eyes glistened with tears, Ann spoke with clarity and composure as she stared down the camera to address her sister's killer directly. 'Michelle was a young girl,' she said. 'You may have a sister the same age. You've raped other women possibly the same age as your mother. I can't believe what you've done to our family. Nothing's going to bring Michelle back. We want you to give yourself up and for anybody with information to come forward. This man has got to be stopped.'

Such was the raw power of this appeal that it was splashed on the front pages of several local newspapers. DI Hill's rebuke had its desired effect, and Walthamstow's phantom stranger rapist was served with a new moniker: the E17 Night Stalker.

Still, no credible leads emerged. Weeks bled into months, and media interest waned. The sad reality was that Michelle's case was just one of 131 murders in London that year.[6] By now, all but the core team dedicated to Michelle's murder had been pulled elsewhere, including Steve. He was reassigned to other cases, including the hammer-killing of a father by his own son in

Poplar, East London. 'No detective likes leaving a case before it's resolved,' said Steve, adding, 'We never forgot about Michelle or her family, but the murder beat in London is nonstop; every team had its own caseload.'

On the first anniversary of Michelle's death, the family arranged for a park bench to be placed by the climbing frame in the playground where she died. It's still there today, bearing the words: *In memory of Michelle Samaraweera. An angel on earth, now an angel in heaven. God bless.*[7]

Another six months went by.

By now, Steve had been brought back onto the Michelle Samaraweera team, this time as case officer, responsible for the day-to-day management of operations, from supervising lines of inquiry to managing evidence and witnesses. 'We wanted to get the message out to a larger area,' he told me. 'One of our ideas was to post leaflets with a CCTV image and photofit of the guy, offering a £20,000 reward to anyone with information that led to his arrest. We had 60,000 printed in several languages, and sent to every business and residential address in the Waltham Forest borough.'

There are no miracles in policing; only in crime dramas. But what happened next felt as close to a *deus ex machina* as a real-life detective gets.

On the morning of 10 November 2010, the hotline phone at murder command HQ rang. It was the owner of a dry-cleaning business in Westminster. He gave his name as Kashif and said he had seen one of the leaflets and recognised the man in the CCTV image. Well, it wasn't his face he recognised; it was the black jacket with two white stripes.

'The guy just said, "I know him, he used to work for me",' said Steve. 'We couldn't believe it. I mean, from 60,000 leaflets, we got just one phone call. One! But sometimes, that's all it takes.'

Finally, a full eighteen months after Michelle's death, police could pin a name on their ghost.

—

Aman Vyas was twenty-four years old when he left his small town on the outskirts of New Delhi for London in late 2007. The son of a retired schoolteacher and housewife, he flew to Britain on a student visa – although he apparently had little intention of studying. Already a university graduate from his time in India, he illegally took a job as one of Kashif's dry-cleaning assistants in September 2008. Police uncovered several associated addresses for him around that time, all in southern Walthamstow, including that of a girlfriend, a local woman with whom he was in a steady relationship by the time of Michelle's murder. One of them was mine.

But there was a problem. According to Kashif, Vyas was no longer in Britain. Suspiciously, airline records revealed that – less than forty-eight hours after the Crimewatch appeal aired – he had bought a one-way ticket to Delhi, on 1 July 2009. Fishier still, he had not only paid for the ticket in cash but had given the Westminster dry cleaner as his home address, rather than let slip where he actually lived in Walthamstow. 'He realised the net was closing, panicked and fled straight back to India on the first flight he could get,' said Steve.

This constituted an even bigger problem: without Vyas in custody, police had no way of sampling his DNA. Without that, they could not incontrovertibly place him at the scene of any of the attacks, a link they would surely need if they had any chance of persuading the notoriously intractable Indian authorities to grant extradition.

Then came another stroke of good fortune. Kashif also employed Vyas's brother, Raja. And he still worked for him. So, a day after he first called police, Kashif pulled from the rubbish a bottle of water that Raja had drunk from and handed it over. Using Raja's saliva on the bottle's rim, forensic investigators were then able to run a 'sibship' test on his DNA. The result was conclusive: Michelle's murderer was a male sibling of the man who had sipped from the bottle. Raja had only one male sibling who had ever been in the UK. It was enough to issue an international arrest warrant.

With the paperwork rubber-stamped, the global manhunt for Vyas began. Airports were on high alert, and Interpol issued a Red Notice, effectively putting him on the watchlist of 194 countries around the world. Tracking him down, however, would require patience, persistence and a degree of international cooperation that can be challenging to secure.

By 2011, inquiries revealed Vyas had been in New Zealand, then Singapore, before the trail went cold. Then, in July 2011, more than two years after the attacks, Indian police called Scotland Yard. They had arrested Vyas at Indira Gandhi Airport in New Delhi as he attempted to fly to Bangkok. From there, it would turn out, his plan was to return to New Zealand, where he had already started a new life with a wife and newborn child.

But this was not the end. For Steve and his team, it was only the start of a new chapter in their fight to bring Vyas to justice.

Indeed, it would take another eight years of international bureaucracy and diplomatic wrangling for the E17 Night Stalker to finally face trial in a British court. For Steve personally, it would become a fight that would consume nearly a decade of his life and stand as a quiet testament to the very best of British police work, a shining example – though few would ever know it – of what dogged determination and meticulous investigation can achieve. 'Ever since I was on the beat as a young PC in West Ham, I never wanted to sit behind a desk taking calls,' Steve said. 'I wanted to be out there, creeping round the streets at 3 a.m. arresting bad people. That was me. I had to be proactive.'

He gulped some coffee, then said: 'And, frankly, when it comes to bad people, it doesn't get worse than Vyas.'

———

Vyas had no intention of facing justice in Britain. Instead, he launched an audacious legal battle, determined to exploit every possible avenue of escape. For eight long years, his legal team waged war in the courtroom, dragging the case through more than fifty hearings. Some days, British media reported, his counsel failed to show up to court or misplaced critical documents. On others, they relentlessly attacked the Metropolitan Police's evidence, portraying it as flimsy and unreliable. In one surprise tactic, they even attempted to shift blame onto Vyas's own brother, Raja. And with a keen eye for loopholes, they tirelessly searched for any legal technicality that might allow Vyas to evade prosecution.

During that time, British media reported that he had been released on bail and was living freely with his family in Delhi. At one point, Steve flew out to the Indian capital to try to convince the authorities how serious they were about bringing Vyas back to Britain. 'He appeared in court maybe once every three or four months, and only ever for about half an hour each time,' he said. 'They'd spend a lot of time talking about the previous hearing, make a little progress, then [the hearing] would be put back again.'

Meanwhile at home, seven years after her death, Michelle's family were beginning to wonder if they would ever see her killer face justice. 'We feel like there's nothing going on,' sister Ann said in 2016. 'It just feels like the whole thing has been left stagnant for the last few years.'[8]

They had to get the story back in the public eye. So, to raise awareness, Ann launched a #Justice4Michelle campaign on social media. The campaign gained momentum and soon caught the attention of Stella Creasy, the Member of Parliament for Walthamstow. Creasy showed her support by leading a women's safety awareness march through the borough in March 2016 for International Women's Day. Then, in April 2018, she brought the case to the highest level of government by directly questioning Prime Minister Theresa May during the weekly televised 'Prime Minister's Questions' session in Parliament.[9]

'In 2009, Michelle Samaraweera was raped and murdered,' Creasy's voice boomed through the House of Commons. 'Since 2012, Aman Vyas has been avoiding extradition for this and eight other charges of sexual violence against women in Walthamstow. There have been forty-seven hearings to date, with the judge not showing up for seven of them, and seven different judges have been appointed. When the prime minister talks to her good friend Prime Minister Modi while he is here in London, will she commit to raising this case with him and asking India to take it seriously, so that we can finally get justice for Michelle?'

The prime minister dodged the question, saying it was 'important that we recognise the independence of the judiciary in both countries'.

———

Steve would never get the chance to meet the man he'd spent the last eight years of his career hunting. In the autumn of 2018, he made the decision to retire from the force he'd served since he was nineteen years old. 'I'd had a long career, a good career, and, you know, I'd done my thirty years and I was ready,' he said. 'And the way things were going in the Indian High Court, there was no knowing when the decision would be made, let alone what it would be. I felt I'd done everything I could for that case, and I knew I'd be leaving it in good hands.'

So, before he left the murder team, Steve handed the case files over to a detective sergeant named Shaleena Sheikh. 'When I first read the files, all I could think was that this is literally every woman's worst nightmare,' she told me in a cafe just outside London. 'Men don't have to look over their shoulder at night or worry about being vulnerable while searching for their keys outside their own front door. But for us, a man like that is the one thing every woman fears most.'

Her eyes turned fierce for a second. 'We absolutely had to get him back.'

The first thing she did when she took over the case was to put a photograph of Michelle on her desk. 'A lot of officers put up pictures of the suspect, but I always felt it was important to remember the people this job is really about,' she said. 'It's so easy to get wrapped up in the hunt for a suspect that you forget not just about the victims but also the families whose lives have been annihilated because of an awful crime. That includes the perpetrator's family. Usually, they're just as innocent.'

Then she added, 'People think being a homicide detective is glamorous. But in reality, it's often just really sad.'

I met Shaleena not long after she'd taken a sabbatical from the force in 2024. She was not the grizzled detective I expected. She arrived in a flowing blue summer dress under a leather jacket and crisp white trainers. Her most striking feature, though, were her eyes, which were huge and kind and penetrating; the sort one imagines have drawn many a confession over the years. She talked quickly and animatedly and with a passion for the job you don't often hear in seasoned police officers.

By the time Shaleena took over the team in 2018, the investigation had already trundled on for eight years. By then, she said, the atmosphere at murder command HQ was one of tired resignation. 'Everybody was saying, "Vyas is never coming back",' she said. 'It had just been going on too long, and nobody thought the decision would go our way.'

But not Shaleena. 'I decided that I wasn't going to stop kicking the hornet's nest,' she said. 'I emailed the Home Office and kept bugging them for updates on what was happening at the hearings. They must have been so fed up with me.'

It paid off. On 15 July 2019, an email pinged in Shaleena's inbox. The Delhi High Court had dismissed all Vyas's petitions for legal protection and granted his extradition to the United Kingdom. 'I must have read that email about ten times to ensure

I understood what it said,' recalled Shaleena. 'I even printed it out and asked a colleague to check it for me. Then it went on the wall next to Michelle's photograph.'

I wanted to know how Steve felt about missing Vyas's extradition; it must have been galling to have, in his words, 'lived and breathed' an investigation for the better part of a decade only to retire two months before the extradition. 'Do I wish I'd hung on a few more months to see it through?' he said. 'Maybe. It was Sod's Law that the decision was made just as I retired. But it was time.'

He looked almost wistful in that moment, then said: 'At the end of the day, I was just glad that the decision came. I was happy for Michelle's family, and for his living victims. They're who all this work, by so many people, was for. For what he put them through, his victims deserved to see that man face justice.'

—

Aman Vyas would become only the third Indian citizen in history to be extradited from India to face criminal charges in the UK.[10] This in itself felt like a coup for the Metropolitan Police. But the job was far from over. The Crown Prosecution Service had already decided that the police's case held enough water to authorise charges. But Shaleena and her team still had the gargantuan task of preparing the case for court. Then, of course, there was the matter of the trial itself.

For a start, the sheer volume of files Steve had left her was staggering: over 900 statements, countless 'exhibit chains', hours of CCTV, mobile phone data, and mountains of DNA evidence. 'Preparing a case of this magnitude for court is an immense undertaking,' Shaleena explained. 'Most cases take up a few shelves at the station. This one had its own storeroom.'

The week leading up to Vyas's return was a blur of anxiety for Shaleena. 'It was a stressful time,' she said. 'We put together an extradition team, who would go out to get him. They travelled all day Monday, on the Tuesday they had to go to a hearing, Wednesday involved various red-tape processes, and on Thursday night they picked him up and flew him back.'

Through all this, Shaleena waited, anxiously following every step of the team's progress. The night of Vyas's return was long and fraught – a night burned black into Shaleena's memory. 'I barely slept,' Shaleena admitted. 'All I could think about was that flight. What if he escapes? What if he's suddenly taken ill? What if there is a crash, or if the plane is subject to a terrorist attack? Whatever could possibly go wrong, I imagined it. So many people had put so much work into this for so long. It was like . . . it almost felt too good to be true.'

Nothing did go wrong. And sure enough, on the morning of 5 October 2019, the plane landed safely, and Shaleena got the call to come to Heathrow. 'I was at the Old Bailey for a trial that morning, but nothing was going to keep me from being there when Vyas was charged,' she said. 'I wanted to charge him personally.'

The first thing she did was text Steve to let him know the good news, then she raced by car to Heathrow police station. When she arrived, Vyas was in a cell, awaiting a visit from his duty solicitor. When that meeting was over, the plan was to then offer him an optional formal interview before filing official charges.

It was evening by the time he walked out of the cell with his lawyer. Far from the hulking monster his violent crimes might suggest, Shaleena remembers a slight and short man with a reedy, unmemorable voice. 'He wasn't at all scary looking,' she recalled. 'He wasn't imposing or threatening. He wasn't even the sort of man most women would cross the street to avoid passing by at night. He looked . . .' She paused to think. 'He looked almost harmless, which makes him all the more dangerous in my view.'

In fact, Shaleena says she cannot remember a single moment when Vyas met her eye that day. 'He wouldn't look at me,' she said. 'When we charged him, he completely refused to engage with me, speaking only to the male officer who was also in the room. And he talked *a lot*. I think he was really put out that a woman was charging him.'

With the charges read out – six counts of rape against four women, one count of grievous bodily harm with intent and one count of murder – Vyas was allowed his phone call. He used it, recalled Shaleena, to telephone his mother in India. Then his photograph was taken, as well as his fingerprints and DNA, which was rushed immediately to forensics to ensure it categorically matched the samples taken from the crime scenes. It did – the odds of it matching another living human being were a billion to one. There was one thing left for Shaleena to do: call Michelle's sister Ann. 'It wasn't about celebrating or jumping for joy. I think it was just relief, really, that some closure to the family's ordeal was finally in sight,' she said.

The next day Vyas appeared at Uxbridge Magistrates' Court where, normally in first court appearances like this, a defendant is required to confirm only their name, address and plea. But Aman Vyas, 'of no fixed abode', had more than that to say. 'He kept talking throughout the hearing,' said Shaleena. 'He kept telling the magistrate that he shouldn't be there, that it was all a big misunderstanding, that there must be someone he can talk to and get it all sorted out. I don't think the magistrate was too happy about all the interruptions.'

For a case of this magnitude, there was no question of where it was heading. After a few minutes, the magistrate committed Vyas to the Crown Court, where he would face trial before a jury of his peers.

—

Eleven years, one month and seven days after Michelle Samaraweera was murdered, Aman Vyas was brought to trial for her rape and murder, as well as the violent rapes of three other women.

Nobody came to support him in Courtroom Seven of Croydon Crown Court on the first day, or any other day, of proceedings. Neither his mother nor father, no brother, no friends, no colleagues. Whether his family wanted to be there or not, international travel restrictions would have presented a significant obstacle; this was one of the first crown court trials to take place since the outbreak of Covid-19, and flights to and from India had been suspended since March.

As another consequence of Covid-19 restrictions, the usually bustling courtroom was abnormally quiet. Attendance was limited only to those who needed to be there, face masks were mandatory, and seating was carefully arranged to maintain a safe distance. Members of Michelle's family were there, together, to see the man they'd waited more than a decade to look in the eye. Barristers, courtroom administrators and involved police officers sat in the well of the court, spaced two metres apart. That's where Shaleena sat every day for the next four weeks to hear, on top of everything else, Vyas's defence – a defence that the presiding judge, Mr Justice Bryan, would later dismiss as a 'cock-and-bull story'.[11]

It is worth outlining his defence here because it reveals a critical insight into the kind of man he is. Here was a defendant who, despite the weight of overwhelming evidence against him, did not simply confess to what he did. Instead, he cavilled and quibbled, resisted and prevaricated, constructing a farrago of distortions that were, at times, almost comical in their delusion. Although I wasn't there to hear it myself, I gleaned the following information from court transcripts released to me by Mr Justice Bryan.

Of the first attack in March 2009, Vyas claimed not that he forced his way into the woman's home, but that she invited him in for consensual sex. He said he then stopped the liaison after seeing a photograph of her late husband and realising she was a widow. In the end, he changed his plea to guilty of her rape, but not to the accompanying violence. This was the only confession any of his victims would hear.

Of the second attack, he denied ever meeting the woman at first. But when prosecuting barrister Tom Little KC asked him to explain his DNA on her underwear, he changed tack, claiming he had in fact visited her at her hostel for consensual sex some weeks prior. But when this claim was refuted by the hostel register, which did not contain his name, he concocted a new story: he had previously had intercourse with two sex workers – whom he could not name, nor say when he had met – on the very same mattress. Somehow, he argued, his DNA must have passed from the mattress onto his victim's underwear when she was later raped by another stranger. 'If this man is innocent, he must be the unluckiest man in the world,' Mr Little told the jury. 'He has to be so unlucky, it just defies belief.'

He claimed no knowledge of the third attack and could give no explanation as to how his DNA found its way onto the red ambulance blanket. Perhaps, he said, he had touched her arm earlier in the night and somehow his DNA had passed from there to the blanket. 'It's important that you use your common sense,' Mr Little reminded the jury. 'Semen doesn't fly. You might be able to flick it, but Walthamstow must have been awash with his semen if he's an innocent man, and it wasn't.'

As for Michelle, Vyas said they'd met a couple of times before and there had been a frisson. So, when he bumped into her outside the Somerfield at 1 a.m. that night, she took him to a bench in the playground to chat. That's when, he claimed, she initiated sex with him on the cold ground. But mid-coitus, he said, she suddenly and inexplicably passed out. Rather than call 999 on his mobile phone, he panicked and fled. Whatever happened to her after that had nothing to do with him, he asserted. CCTV did, after all, record other men in the area that night.

Mr Little gave this argument as short a shrift as he had the others. 'Let's assume there was rapist number two in the area at the same time as this man,' he said. 'Not a copycat of Mr Vyas, just another one. Rather surprising that we don't have his semen, isn't it? I mean, this is just cloud-cuckoo-land from the defendant.'

Vyas hit back with this: even if Michelle had died during sex with him, he didn't mean to kill her. It must, therefore, be manslaughter. 'Men or women would be dying in their thousands in bed, if simply being on top of someone and having . . . intercourse with them would kill them,' said Mr Little, adding, 'This is no manslaughter case. It's murder, all night long.'

In the end, the trial lasted four weeks. In that time the jury heard evidence from Steve Lynch and other officers, various witnesses, a forensic scientist, a pathologist, the paramedic with the red blanket, Kashif the dry cleaner and more. However, Shaleena said the most difficult testimonies to hear were those of Vyas's three living victims. 'I can't imagine how hard that must have been for them,' she said. 'The fact he made them do that, to relive the worst thing that can happen to a woman for the world to hear, just . . . it's beyond words.'

And so, on 31 July 2020, the jury left Courtroom Seven to consider their verdict. When they returned, their decision was unanimous: guilty on all counts.

'In the spring of 2009, there was a stranger rapist prowling the streets of Walthamstow in East London looking for his prey. You were that rapist,' Mr Justice Bryan told Vyas in his lengthy sentencing remarks. 'This series of increasingly violent rapes, which occurred over a relatively short period of time, all took place late at night on women close to both where you and they lived in Walthamstow.' He went on: 'Quite apart from such tragic loss of life, you left behind you a trail of physical and psychological injuries.'

After describing each of Vyas's crimes in, at times excruciating, detail, he added: 'You have shown neither compassion nor remorse for your victims throughout your trial, putting those who were alive, and could remember events, through the ordeal

of reliving events, whilst you continued to protest your inno-
cence to the bitter end, concocting ever more fanciful versions of
events, as you struggled to explain away the weight of the evidence
against you.'

The most powerfully excoriating words, however, were left to
Michelle's sister, Ann, who had sat in court every day since the
trial began.[12] 'Aman Vyas has had over eleven years to come clean
and admit to raping and murdering my sister, and even longer to
admit to all the other heinous crimes committed against all the
other innocent victims,' she said. 'He has also had all this time to
reflect on his own life and address the issues that have turned him
into a monster.

'Instead, he has lied and fabricated stories for his own benefit.
He will never understand what he put my mother, sisters, children,
loved ones, friends and myself through. Vyas potentially spending
the rest of his life in prison is not a punishment but a privilege, it
will never be enough.'

Then, in a moment of raw and remarkable humanity, she
turned to Vyas himself and said: 'There's a glimmer of sadness
there as well. You weren't born that way, something's turned you
into what you are.'

To this, I am told, Vyas offered no discernible reaction.

On 20 August 2020, Mr Justice Bryan issued his sentence:
a minimum of thirty-seven years in prison, minus time already
served, with no possibility of early parole.

Then, when everything was said that could be said, the E17
Night Stalker was led away to begin life in his new home: a grey
concrete prison cell in the north of England where he would live
at least until 2055. Or, possibly, for the rest of his life.

Chapter 8

THE JOURNEY BEGINS

Lisa stood in the doorway, wrinkling her nose as she surveyed the living room. 'Wow, you've painted,' she said. 'Very pink, isn't it?'

She'd come over to pick up Jasmine for the first time since I'd moved in; our daughter was upstairs playing teachers to an unruly class of cuddly toys. It was a fine day in May and the sun streamed in, giving the living room a bright look. Lisa was wearing blue jeans and a green silk blouse. She had a new haircut. I watched her walk over to a picture on the far wall and straighten it with one hand. 'That's better,' she murmured. I hated how good she looked.

'I thought it would brighten up the place,' I managed. 'But now I'm not sure. The paint recycling centre was selling it cheap. It's called Nancy's Blushes, but Jody says it reminds her of nappy rash.'

Lisa chuckled, though she looked uncomfortable. Then she shuddered. A stitch of concern had sewn itself between her eyes. 'Matt, I'm happy you're moving on. But I have to say, the place feels . . .'

She paused.

'What?' I asked, pertly.

'It feels heavy. Stagnant. And what's that smell? Is it drains? Or damp?'

I nodded, unable to meet her eyes. 'I don't know. I've been feeling it too.'

Lisa's gaze shifted about the room and her face softened. 'I don't know, it just has kind of a . . . I don't know, something I can't quite . . .'

'A what?' I butted in.

'I don't know, Matt. Like, a strange vibe.'

I didn't respond immediately. I wanted to share. After more than a decade together it was a hard habit to break. But I still blamed her for the divorce, and for forcing me into living in this house, alone. *She doesn't deserve to know anything about my life,* I thought.

Then I heard myself saying, 'There was an incident here a while back.'

Her eyes widened. 'What kind of incident?'

I took a breath. 'Nothing really,' I said, trying to sound nonchalant. 'I just found out there were a few fires here, and that a murderer apparently lived here about ten years ago.'

Lisa gasped. 'Oh my god, Matt! You're living in a murder house?'

'Well, not really. No one was killed inside the house. He just lived here for a bit.'

She was silent for a moment, digesting the information. 'And you're letting Jasmine stay here?'

'It was before we moved in,' I said. 'I'm going to replace the burned floorboards, and the guy is long gone. He's in prison.'

Lisa's face soured into a familiar frown of disapproval. She shook her head. 'Matt, I don't know about this. I don't want Jasmine exposed to any . . . negative energy.'

'Negative energy?' I scoffed. 'Come on, Lisa. You don't believe in that stuff.'

But even as I said it, I recalled the strange sense of unease that had been growing inside me since I moved in. That creeping, slithering sensation that something wasn't quite right in here.

Lisa's eyes now brimmed with worry. 'I do, Matt. And I think you should too. Have you burned sage?'

I blinked, caught off guard. 'Sage?'

'Yeah. It's supposed to clear out negative energy.' She paused, then added with a tentative smile, 'I could come back later and do it for you, if you want.'

I was strangely touched. Though, childishly, I wasn't about to let her know that. And like all freshly separated parents, I suppose, it was a good day when we managed to ignore the herd of elephants in the corner of the room.

I shifted up into arsehole gear. 'You know I'm not into that sh—'

But I stopped myself and she flashed a magnanimous smile. 'Well, if you ever change your mind, I'd be happy to do it. I can drop off a few crystals too, if you like. To help with the cleansing.'

I felt sure she was winding me up. She'd always been a little New-Agey, which I used to find kookily attractive. But the crystals thing was new. Then, maybe she was right. Maybe a waft of smoke and a prayer could cleanse this place of whatever darkness may or may not be in its walls. It couldn't harm, could it?

'I'll think about it,' I conceded.

She nodded, her smile ripening. 'Okay. And hey,' she reached out to touch my arm, 'if that doesn't work, maybe we can find you a good priest.'

Now I knew she was having a laugh. *A priest!* That was the second time that word had come up in recent weeks. It was a desperate measure. I hadn't been to church since the 1994 Islington Scout Remembrance Parade, not counting a couple of funerals. I'm not religious. I don't believe in God. But maybe I *was* desperate. I forced a weak smile and nodded. 'Very funny,' I said.

Outside the wind was picking up, hurrying the clouds across the sky and ushering a plastic carrier bag across the street. As I watched Lisa and Jasmine drive away, a breath of dread wafted over me. I felt the house's gaze on my back. This wasn't over, not by a long shot. I turned back into the empty living room and pulled out my phone. My fingers hovered over the screen as I debated my next move. Then, with a deep breath, I typed in the search bar: *Exorcists near me.*

—

I lost my faith on the day Will Jack killed Father Christmas for me. Will was a lanky seven-year-old who loved cars and being right. It was December 1990, Blue Class at Hanover Primary School, Islington. We were sitting around the art table making Christmas cards for our parents with poster paint and glue that smelled like fish bones. I can still picture Will unfolding out of his chair to tower over the group, then sneer: 'He's not real, you know, Father Christmas. I know he's not real because my sister told me. She says it's just a story our parents tell to make kids behave.'

It was a shattering moment. The world suddenly looked so . . . small. It all seemed so obvious. No Santa must mean no tooth fairy. If no fairies at the end of the garden, then surely no angels in the clouds. And if no angels, then what? There's an all-knowing, all-seeing old man in the sky who'll grant you wishes if you behave but cast you into an eternal fire if you don't? My parents mixed up the names of their own sons at times, and there were only three of us. How could God be on prayer-granting terms with 2.4 billion individual Christians all at once?

We never went to church growing up. My father's severe Catholic upbringing combined with my mother's medical-grade atheism to ensure that would never happen. As I grew, I began to notice the Church's contradictions, its puzzling rules and inherent implausibility. The funny clothes, the incense and ceremony wafting you up, up and away to another, infinitely better-smelling place. By my teens I'd become a hardened rationalist, convinced that God was a fairy tale for grown-ups and that religion was a tool of control.

—

The internet is not short of 'spirit removal services'. Within about five minutes of searching, I had scrolled through half a dozen sites with titles ranging from the witchy ('Your life is guided by a roadmap of stars') to the straight-to-business ('Evil Spirit Removal | 100% Result | Affordable Fee'). One site even offered among its services – on top of 'removal of evil spirit from house' – to 'get [my] love back', 'fix broken relationship' and 'solution for court cases'.

Before long, one website caught my eye. It was called The Dr. Wanda Pratnicka Center and specialised in 'spirit attachment removal'.[1] It was the top sponsored site on Google's rankings and, judging by its design, appeared to have turned the practice of spirit cleansing into an industrial operation.

Its head office was apparently in New York but it had hotlines for the afflicted in Britain, Canada and Australia too. Its website was white and crisp, full of high-resolution stock photos of good-looking people with their heads in their hands, and statements like 'Over the past 50 years we have helped 10,000+ people around the world recover from emotional disturbances and physical illnesses that in many cases were considered incurable.'

Its 'haunted houses' page wasn't hard to find.

'We receive many phone calls and emails each week from people who believe that there are spirits in their home,' it revealed. 'But after taking a closer look, we find that spirits have already possessed them. People often try to get rid of spirits using holy water, smudging, burning white candles, Feng Shui, or rice and salt. In most cases, we find these methods to be unsuccessful.'

If I wanted to learn more, it said I had to buy the founder's book for £15.95. I clicked on the 'service' page. 'Spirit attachment removal' was something it said it had developed over fifty years ago to liberate 'astral entities from a distance'. So, no one would ever actually come to my house? Not necessary, the sales pitch said. All they'd need was my first and last name, my date of birth and my address. The rest would be done remotely, it said.

'It doesn't matter where the client is located in order to successfully remove spirits from them. It's more effective from a remote distance because it makes the process more peaceful and prevents spirits from fighting back.' There was no mention of exactly how the remote cleanse worked. Just that it did.

It was all beginning to feel a little oily. Then I found the 'packages' page and learned that a twelve-week spirit attachment removal programme cost between £395 and £1,195 depending on the package I chose. The more you paid, the more caseworker calls you got, as well as more books by the company's founder.

I knew what I needed to do. I closed the window and Googled: *Church of England deliverance ministry.*

Chapter 9

THE EXORCIST

It's almost as if the Church of England's deliverance ministry webpage doesn't want to be found. After some searching, I found it tucked inside the 'mental health resources' section of the Church's wider website.[1] It is clean and crisp, much like website of The Dr. Wanda Pratnicka Center. Unlike that website, however, it contains a lot of information about mental health, safeguarding, modern slavery and so on – nothing about possessive spirits or haunted houses at all. It's as sober a place you'll find on the internet, a sort of online equivalent to a therapist's waiting room.

'Deliverance ministry is a specialist ministry within the Church of England and constitutes one aspect of the Church of England's commitment to bringing wholeness, peace and healing to all who experience distress, whether in body, mind or spirit,' it stated.

I dug deeper. Finally, I unearthed a PDF entitled 'safeguarding e-manual'. Here, sandwiched between 'domestic abuse' and 'spiritual abuse' was a section on 'deliverance ministry' – the Church's good practice guide for ministers engaging with the 'ministry of liberating, freeing, or delivering a person from a burden which they carry'.

On the subject of exorcism, it simply said: 'Christian exorcism is a specific act in which an imperative or invocatory appeal to Christ or to the Godhead is made in order to rid a person or place of an evil spirit by which they are possessed. It is the "binding and releasing", the "casting out" or "expelling" of an evil or malevolent possessing spirit that is not human.'

'If you or someone you know would like to discuss deliverance ministry, please contact your parish priest,' the website said.

—

Dear Reverend,

My name is Matt Blake and I live in your parish.

An unusual one, this, perhaps. But do you have a moment to discuss deliverance ministry with me? I've recently experienced some unsettling events at home, and the CofE's deliverance ministry webpage says I should first contact my local priest. That's you. There's something else: I have also learned of some rather unpleasant details about my house's past that might be relevant.

I'm happy to visit the church whenever it suits your schedule.

Sincerely,

Matt

Weeks passed, no reply. I was beginning to wonder if the Church of England even has a ministry that deals with the supernatural. Then, finally, I found a priest far away from my own parish, but one for whom exorcism was an actual job. More than just a parish priest, Dr Jason Bray was one of the Anglican Church's most senior, and sought-after, deliverance ministers.

—

Picture in your mind what an Anglican exorcist should look like. It's more than probable you're imagining Dr Jason Bray. In the same way you would expect a 1980s hair-metal guitarist to be all tattoos and perm, a butcher to have a bloody apron, or an AI specialist to be completely dead behind the eyes, Dr Bray is the living embodiment of a man who delivers demons from the powers of darkness for a living. And no, if you're wondering, he says he has never seen *The Exorcist*.

When he's on the job, he only wears black. Over his clericals, he often wears a black ankle-length overcoat, beneath a black trilby to complete the look. He goes nowhere without his dark leather satchel, in which he carries the tools of his trade: a bunch of spare crucifixes, a vial of holy water and, of course, a Bible (no, really, he says he's never watched *The Exorcist* in his life). It's easy to imagine him poring over ancient books in dimly lit libraries, or tracing holy symbols in the air, his fingers leaving trails of shimmering light that repel encroaching darkness. Except, in his words, his work as a deliverance minister is 'more like the gas man than your conventional Hollywood exorcist'.

'My day job, if you like, is just your classic Anglican vicar,' he told me. 'I do all the things normal vicars do, like Sunday service and christenings, weddings, funerals and pastoral care. Only, I'm also a member of the Church's deliverance ministry with special permission, and training, to deal with the paranormal.'

In the UK, it is very difficult to get clergy to speak openly about this subject. It's a wing of the Church that has for many years been – in Jason's words – 'veiled in secrecy'. The general wisdom for this has always been that deliverance is not a joke and should be done with 'a minimum of publicity'.

Then, one of his cases involving a Muslim family and the ghost of a Christian monk found its way into the national press.[2] It was, he said, roundly misinterpreted and led to a fever of tabloid attention. As a result, Church top brass decided deliverance was 'something the Church should talk about a bit more'. So they gave Jason the green light to write a book about his experiences. It's called *Deliverance: Everyday Investigations into Poltergeists, Ghosts and Other Supernatural Phenomena by an Anglican Priest*.[3] It is warm, witty and wise, and a great read.

'I think whatever reservations I had about talking publicly about deliverance were knocked out of me after the book came out,' he emailed before we met. 'Nothing has been the same since being interviewed live on *This Morning* by Holly and Phil, of blessed memory.'

Jason, who has been vicar of St Giles' Church in Wrexham for the past decade, said he didn't have time to meet me in person because he was busy preparing to change jobs – he'd recently been promoted to Dean of Llandaff Cathedral in Cardiff. But he agreed to a video call from his office.

Not anyone can become a deliverance minister. You have to be a vicar first. Then, if the chips fall right, you must be appointed by a bishop who oversees all your work. Then you are sent on a comprehensive training programme where you delve deep into scripture, hone your counselling skills, and learn the intricacies of spiritual liberation. You learn to discern spiritual needs, navigate the complexities of deliverance practices, and collaborate with other clergy and professionals. Critically, you must also develop a keen understanding of mental health.

There's another thing you need to carry out this job: proper insurance. Here's where the Ecclesiastical Insurance Group comes in, providing specialist cover should anything go awry in the casting-out of evil. I assumed this is to provide cover for when, say, an evil spirit flings you down a flight of stairs like Father Karras in *The Exorcist*. In fact, the reason is far more pragmatic. 'If it's generally known that a house has been "exorcised", then the price of the house may drop, which would mean that the minister might be sued for the difference,' he explains in his book.

—

To call Jason a real-life ghostbuster is broadly accurate (he laughs at the association), but also reductive. Because to him, the Church and to the 27.5 million self-identified Christians (of all denominations) across England and Wales,[4] deliverance is a serious business. 'I think a lot of people assume what I do is all about Ouija boards and swivelling heads and floating beds,' he told me. 'But it is much less exciting than that most of the time.'

Still, when Jason talks about life in the deliverance game, he talks in the measured, slightly faraway tone of a man who's been around the crypt and back again. He's seen things most people don't. Heard things many people can't. His voice is soft and deep and puts you quickly at ease. A tool of the trade. On the day we met, he was smartly dressed. White 'dog collar', black blazer. Short grey hair persuaded into a neat parting. He has a kind face – another useful tool.

In many ways, Jason sees his role as more detective than ghost botherer. 'My job is often to get to the bottom of what is causing the disturbance. It could be an actual ghost, or a poltergeist, or it could be something much more mundane and explainable,' he said, adding with a chuckle, 'Sometimes it's just a case of someone letting their imagination run wild.'

Then, of course, there is mental illness. In fact, mental health is so common a factor in the home visits Jason carries out that he is regularly in touch with several community psychiatric nurses in his area. It's a delicate act. 'It is the toughest part of the job,' he said, a little wearily. 'I'd say about half of all the visits I do end with me recommending that they go to see their GP. Social Services are often involved.'

One time, Jason took a call about a woman plagued by phantom rats. Night after night she woke up to find her body crawling with rodents as they feasted on her flesh. Her daughter even backed up the story, claiming to have witnessed a 'seething mass of bodies' under the covers. 'It was like I could hear them too, chattering to one another, as they were eating her alive,' she told Jason at the time. '[But] when I pulled back the bedclothes they were gone.'

It got creepier. When Jason arrived to bless the house, the kitchen spotlights suddenly began to pop, one by one. 'I've never been more terrified than I was in that moment,' he recalls. But there was something they hadn't told him: the older woman had been awaiting the results of a bowel cancer test. His conclusion? She'd somehow externalised her fear of cancer, so her imagination created the rats as a gruesome metaphor for the disease she felt was eating her from the inside out. As for her daughter, she'd become so caught up in the shared terror, she may have experienced a kind of empathetic hallucination.

And the lights? 'They'd put the wrong bulbs in,' he said. 'They overheated. A coincidence.'

He's also met his share of people with schizophrenia convinced they were being followed by shadows that weren't their own, or people so lonely their imaginations created 'entities' to keep them company. One elderly woman, whose husband was not long dead, believed her vaginal soreness was being caused by an incubus (or male sex ghost) descending upon her each night to make non-consensual spectral love.

But this isn't to say Jason hasn't seen his share of The Real Thing. He believes most hauntings are less Hollywood block-buster, more low-budget indie flick: nuanced, unpredictable and quietly terrifying. He's visited houses where ornaments have spontaneously exploded and homes filled with 'a pervading sense of clammy gloom' that instantly vanished as he recited the Lord's Prayer, sending a pulse of energy through his body before a 'tangible warmth' filled the room.

—

We discussed a few of these stories. Then we got to mine. After I explained, he sat silently for a moment. He nodded. He squinted faintly. Then he asked something I wasn't expecting. 'Was there a child at the house when any of these things were happening?'

I was taken aback. 'Why?'

'Because sometimes children are more attuned to this than others,' he said. 'And particularly the divorce, that would have been traumatic for her.'

'I think it was,' I said. 'I think it still is.'

I thought back to the nights of strange things. Jason was right – Jasmine had been in the house each time something had happened. The radio, the doorbell. She'd been in bed, asleep, on every occasion. Then again, this was her home too.

'But what's her trauma got to do with phantom radios and doorbells?' I asked.

Did Jason's denim-blue eyes just betray the flicker of impatience? Don't think so. They met mine.

'Well, it could be poltergeist activity.'

'A poltergeist?' I repeated.

'It's one possible explanation,' he said. 'Poltergeist activity is always caused by somebody alive and present who is usually undergoing some kind of trauma or stress that they're unable to communicate. This can result in things moving around, like kitchen utensils or shoes. I don't see why that couldn't include radios or doorbells.'

'Sort of like a physical projection of a person's anxiety?' I said.

'Exactly. Poltergeists are not ghosts. I have experienced poltergeists myself and heard many, many people describe them to me. And the really strange thing is that children or teenagers seem particularly susceptible.'

'Why?'

'Basically, it is most often associated with people who struggle, or are unable, to express themselves, or who haven't yet developed the emotional language to release whatever trauma they're experiencing,' he said. 'In your daughter's case, it's possible that any anxiety she has over the divorce could be manifesting itself as poltergeist activity.'

I wondered if it was anything like Roald Dahl's Matilda, from the book of the same name, who develops telekinetic powers as a response to her miserable homelife.

'I suppose that is one way to look at it, except you can't control a poltergeist,' he said. 'The theory is that frustration builds up inside a person until the mind or body cannot contain it any longer. Then, finally, that energy bursts out into the world.' He told me to think of it like lightning in a thunderstorm. The build-up of negative emotions inside a person is like the gathering of electrical charges in a cloud. These emotions seek release, similar to the charged particles searching for a path to the ground. The environment around the person, especially if it's already tense or emotionally charged, acts as a conduit, drawing out the pent-up energy. Then, when the internal and external forces connect, a sudden burst of energy is released, manifesting as poltergeist activity – the 'lightning bolt' of emotions.

It might be the way Jason's voice draws you in, like a campfire on a cold evening under the stars. But, in the moment, this all seemed very reasonable.

'Of course, it could also be you,' he said.

'Me?'

'You haven't told your daughter about the house's past, have you?'

'She wouldn't understand.'

'I can imagine divorce has been hard on you. The move, solo parenting. Add that to what you have learned about your house's past, and I would suggest that somehow, subconsciously, you could be picking up on the fact that there is something wrong with this house and that becomes manifest through your energy.'

An interval of silence followed. I could feel the warmth of his empathy. I could understand why he'd been doing this job for so long. 'I sometimes feel as if the house is making me unhappy,' I heard myself say.

'Well, there is something else to consider,' he said. 'You could be experiencing some sort of place memory. Have you done any building work?'

'Some.'

'Building work can trigger place memory.'

'Place memory?'

'It's essentially when a house or piece of ground replays something that has happened there in the past,' he said.

A place memory is not what Jason describes as a 'true haunting' – no troubled souls calling out from the dark beyond. Those are very rare indeed, in his experience. There is no attempt at communication in place memory. Rather, according to him, it is more like a residual echo or imprint of a past event. A psychic snapshot burned onto the environment. The example he uses in his book is of a fox hunt bursting through the pub wall to the terror of late-night drinkers. It can also be something traumatic, like a previous homeowner falling down the stairs and breaking his neck, causing present-day occupants to feel a need to 'step over' him.

'A friend of mine not long ago moved into a new vicarage, where his study was freezing all the time,' recalled Jason. 'It made no sense. It wasn't north facing, was well insulated, good windows. But no matter how high he turned up the heating it never got any warmer. Not just cold, an oppressive chill. Then his grandson suggested sprinkling holy water about the place to bless the house. As he did this, he said he literally could feel the cold lift like a fog and the room was warm. It later turned out that several vicars who'd lived there had suffered mental breakdowns in the house. And as a vicar, if you're going to have a breakdown, it's going to be in the study. That's basically your space.'

He glanced around his own study, then added, 'It's as if the house, that particular room, had absorbed all the angst and unhappiness from a whole load of people in the past. And that physically impacted the atmosphere of the room.'

Could this really be what was happening to me? Could Vyas's presence in the house have left an imprint on its *genius loci*? Or could it be that the very knowledge of his presence here created a build-up of anxious energy inside me that I've projected onto the house? 'Or it could be a combination of all those things,' Jason said.

'But . . . but how?'

—

Jason is not a scientist. He'll be the first to tell you that's not his job. His job is not to offer explanations for these phenomena, or to look for holes in the 2,000-odd years of teaching that have led him to where he is now. His job, he'll tell you, is primarily to help people in his community to live fuller, happier lives. In his business, people don't turn to a priest for 'hows', only 'whys'.

'I don't know what physical mechanisms cause place memory, or poltergeists or ghosts,' he said. 'But it makes sense from my point of view because I deal with this stuff all the time. I've experienced it. So, in a sense, it is a framework by which I can rationalise other people's experiences. And it does seem to work.'

Once, after performing a guest service at Cambridge University, he asked a physicist if there were any scientific framework through which to understand paranormal activity. 'He said, "I can work out quantum physics, I understand string theory, and even the theoretical possibility of time travel, but stuff moving around without you touching it? It doesn't make any sense at all."'

For the first time I detected the ghost of a smile beginning to haunt the edges of Jason's eyes. 'What I do isn't magic, but sometimes it looks like it is,' he said.

'If it's not magic, then how would you explain that to a sceptic?' I said.

He didn't need to think about his answer. 'Obviously I'm a Christian. I believe that God works in the world and that he answers prayers and that [deliverance] is basically a formalised prayer. It is a way of inviting God to do something about it.'

His face had stretched into a full smile now. 'How it works with holy water that's being thrown everywhere . . . well . . . I don't know.'

He let out a laugh, and added, 'It just does.'

Chapter 10

THE EMPTY SHOWER

In the dream, I'm usually in bed. The first thing I feel is the heat. It moves quickly through the room, stealing my breath as it catches my lungs. It's dry and rising. I peel open my eyes and squint through the dark. I'm trying to make sense of it. The edges of the room flicker with an orange glow, casting ghastly dancing shadows in the murk. I can hear it then – the guttural growl of the fire.

Flames are curling up the walls, around the furniture, along the bookshelf. Black smoke writhes against the ceiling, searching for an escape route. It rolls above the bed and banks down the walls, billowing tendrils reaching out, hunting. It's hunting for more air to devour, more space to consume. I can't see. I can't move.

I try to heave myself up to get out. But I'm pinned to the bed, as if an invisible weight is pressing hard against my chest. All I can do is watch the inferno tear through the room. It's licking the walls and blistering the paint in blotches that gurgle and drip onto the blackening floorboards. Plants fizz into ash. Photographs of happy memories bubble and melt. Windows pop. *Bang!* The bed is an island in a sea of fire. *Bang.* The ceiling is crawling down the walls and the floor is crawling up to meet it. *Bang. Bang.*

Then I hear her scream: 'Daddy! Daddy!' It's Jasmine's voice – high-pitched and terrified. 'Heeelp me.'

I scream back hoarsely, but the flames drown out my cries. I want to get to her but I still can't move. The heat is becoming unbearable, scorching my skin, burning my lungs. The flesh on my arms is beginning to blister like the photographs on the bedside table. I try to scream for help, but there is no voice in my mouth. Just smoke. The fire is roaring with an open-throated hunger. That's all I can hear now. There are no sirens in the distance, no shouts from outside. I know no one is coming. *No one is coming!*

—

I've had nightmares before. But these ones were sharper around the edges than others I remembered. Crisper in the mind. They didn't happen every night. And they weren't always the same. Sometimes I was in the bedroom. Sometimes I was outside the house clawing at the windows to get in. But there was always a fire. And there was always the house. When I had it, this nightmare clung to me through the day like a smell.

I didn't tell anybody about this. A wise man once said – actually, it was Adrian Mole in *The Secret Diary of Adrian Mole Aged 13 ¾* – 'There's only one thing more boring than listening to other people's dreams, and that's listening to their problems.'[1]

But I had problems, too. And they seemed to be getting worse.

It had been more than six months since I'd moved in. And yet, when night seeped in, the house seemed to awaken. It wasn't just the creaking floorboards and sighing pipes – the usual bedtime routine of an ageing house settling down for the night.

I began to hear distinct sounds coming from upstairs. The heavy thud of a door slamming shut. Measured footsteps on the stairs. The creak of heavy furniture being dragged across a floor. It wasn't just me; Jody heard them too.

So, we followed Louis's lead and invented a ghost to joke about. We called him Gary – Gary the Ghost. We imagined Gary clanking impotently around empty rooms like Oscar Wilde's Canterville Ghost.[2] 'Oops, Gary's having an early night,' we'd say to a muffled thump. Or, 'Gary's in a huff tonight. Must've forgotten to oil his chains again.'

It was less easy to laugh when I was alone. Most of the time, I attributed the noises to the thin walls of old houses. *A neighbour stomping up the stairs next door,* I'd reassure myself. Though there were times it happened when I knew the neighbours weren't home because I'd accepted their parcels that day. Times when I was sure the sound was not coming from left or right . . . but above or below. I found myself obsessively closing doors and windows when I left rooms and squinting up dark staircases for moving shadows. Nothing ever revealed itself. And yet, the noises continued. On more than one occasion, I found a door ajar when I was sure I'd left it shut. If I didn't know better, I'd have sworn someone else was in the house with me. Of course, I knew better.

Soon, the tapping started.

It was subtle, barely audible at first. Not so loud that it's all you can hear, but loud enough that it'd infuriate anyone with something else to listen to. And once I'd noticed it, I couldn't train my ears on anything else.

Even with the television turned up high I could make it out: a hollow and irregular tick-ticking, somewhere in the room. It sounded at times like Morse code, like a muffled rhythm of dots and dashes tapping out a message I didn't know how to decipher.

I suddenly became overwhelmingly aware of the depth and impenetrability of the shadows that pooled about the corners of the house, even when the lights were on.

After putting Jasmine to bed, I'd spend hours alone in the darkness downstairs, listening. Pressing a glass to my ear, I hunted those noises around the living room – along walls, behind radiators, beneath floorboards. But whenever I thought I'd found one, it would stop. Then it would restart elsewhere.

Some nights they never came. On others, it felt as though the house was closing in around me. It was as if the walls, or something deep within them, were whispering to me. Of course, I knew they weren't whispering because houses don't speak. Bricks are not sentient. Wood does not think. Plasterboards don't judge. Wiring doesn't gaslight. Even so, when it got dark – and there were nights when it got very dark – I grew certain that the house *was* whispering.

I hadn't heard a whisper in days when it happened. I was asleep. I was always asleep when the house really tried to frighten me. There were no dreams in this sleep. It was shallow and thin, just like the sliver of moon breathing its sickly light in through the window.

The sound was jarring. I stirred, unsure if it was part of a dream I'd already forgotten. I rolled over and pulled the covers up to my shoulders. The room was freezing. But the sound was building. It was a rushing sound, hissing and ethereal, like the distant whooshing of a Tube train pushing air through a tunnel before emerging at the platform.

Then, as my senses realigned with reality, I realised. It was the unmistakable rush of water. It was coming from the bathroom.

Foggy from sleep, I dragged myself out of bed and stumbled towards the source. My feet were heavy on the balding carpet. The darkness oozed over me, as if weighted down by something heavier than night. The room groaned and shifted, settling into its happiest state – still, black and spiteful.

Looking back, it should've been obvious what it was. But in the moment, I hadn't a clue. The sound was strangely magnetic, pulling me in.

I pushed the door open. My heart, by now, was drumming in my ears, almost drowning out the sound. And there it was: the shower running at full blast. It wasn't just trickling or dribbling, as showers do after you turn them off. It was a torrent. A sloosh. A full-on gush of water. It was like something – or someone – was having a shower.

But nothing was having a shower. The faucet wasn't in the 'on' position. The shampoo bottle wasn't floating mid-air, squirting onto an invisible head. I stood there and watched the water cascading violently into the shower pan, its droplets catching the moonlight and scattering it across the room in a wild dance. The sight was mesmerising, as if the water was alive. I reached out my hand and ran it through the falling water. To my surprise it felt . . . not quite hot, but warm.

I was rooted to the spot, my mind frothing with questions. Had I forgotten to turn it off? No, that was impossible. I hadn't showered that day. And I'd been away at Jody's for the three days before that. Was it a malfunction? Something to do with the water pressure? *It has to be something to do with the water pressure.*

A plumber would have a perfectly reasonable explanation. But what if they didn't? What if it was something else?

And then, with a throaty splutter, the shower stopped dead. The silence that followed was mighty, thickened by the slow pip-pip of a few dying drips.

With a shiver, I retreated to my bedroom, the water still rushing between my ears. But I didn't fall back to sleep. I just lay there in the thick, silent night, feeling more alone than I'd ever felt before. I could feel tears swimming down my cheeks, soaking the pillow. I wanted to scream. I wanted to get out. I wanted to run away from this house and from my life and start again in another city. Another country.

This was where I'd come to. I was falling through the darkness. I had been for months, ever since I'd moved here. The further I fell, flailing through the black air, the more I felt as though the house was part of it. The slugs, the mice, the radio, the doorbell, the shower, the sounds, the smells . . . its past.

The house has to be part of it, I said to myself. *Because this isn't me. This isn't normal. I know these things can all happen. But not all at once. Not like this. Not in such a short space of time. What the fuck is going on?*

My anxieties were steadily boiling over. They had already begun to foam into my personal life, too. This was manifesting, particularly, in the shape of growing, unsubstantiated feelings of hatred towards my ex-wife. I didn't miss her so much as resent her, which was almost definitely the same thing. I loved her. *No, I don't love her. I don't miss her.* I missed an old version of her, the version I knew before the relationship withered. Or maybe what I really missed was the old version of me – a version that wasn't afraid of the dark, or of the future, or of a pile of old bricks.

It set off a lassitude inside me that curdled my enthusiasm for work and life. I became irascible and reckless. I exploded one of my oldest male friendships in a row over a builder's contact details that went too far. A lucrative freelance writing gig slipped through my fingers because I took too long worrying about the appropriate email response. I got punched in the street because I told a cyclist to fuck off when I stumbled through his bike lane, drunk.

It was almost as if the house itself was making me sick. It was like . . . I felt lighter when I went outside. Healthier, more hopeful.

I knew the house wasn't haunted because *ghosts aren't real*. If anything, I was the haunted one. *Haunted by the house.*

The only ghost in here was me.

—

'You're not seriously telling me you think the house is fucking with you,' said Nick as he made us both coffee in his kitchen a few days after the shower moment.

Nick's house is lovely. It's about a ten-minute walk from mine and about the same size and period. It's usually untidy, littered with toys and other detritus of a busy working family with two young kids and a cat. But it is well lit and airy and always full of life. Plus, he has a very nice coffee machine that does cappuccinos.

'The plumber came round this morning,' I said, 'and he couldn't find anything wrong with the system. He says pressure can cause showers to run but not for as long as a minute, at full force. And warm. I'm telling you. The house is doing some weird shit.'

Nick looked at me as if my words were getting lost in the air between us.

'Maybe he just didn't want to admit he couldn't figure it out,' he said. 'Old houses, old plumbing, weird stuff happens.'

I could feel the frustration rising into my cheeks. 'It's not just the shower. It's the radio turning on by itself, the doorbell ringing with nobody there.'

'Maybe you sleepwalked and turned it on yourself, then went back to bed without knowing,' he said.

'Nick, we shared a bedroom for most of our childhoods. Have you ever seen me sleepwalk? I've never sleepwalked in my life.'

'Then maybe you need an electrician,' Nick shrugged. 'Are you sure you didn't just set the alarm and forgot about it?'

'I didn't even know the radio had an alarm until after it happened. It wasn't set.'

He put down his coffee and gave me a look of mingled sympathy and exasperation. 'Look, mate,' he said. 'I know you're going through a rough time with the divorce and everything, but maybe you're letting your imagination run wild. It's been a stressful year.'

'I'm not imagining it!' I snapped. 'These things really happened.'

He softened his tone. 'I'm not saying you're crazy. But stress can do weird things to your mind. It can fuck with your senses. Maybe you're just extra sensitive right now.'

'The exorcist said it could be me.'

'You spoke to an exorcist?'

I wasn't going to tell Nick about the exorcist. But the words burst out of my mouth like air in a popped balloon. 'Yeah. He said people going through a lot of stress or trauma can project that energy onto their environment and cause things to happen.'

'Is he coming to exorcise your house's demons, then?'

I had considered this. But, after multiple inquiries about deliverance with my local priest failed to draw any kind of response, I chose not to chase it up. 'I don't know,' I said. 'I feel like having a priest come round is basically admitting to myself that ghosts exist. I'm not ready for that yet.'

Nick laughed. I could literally see the sympathy draining from his face. 'Mate, you're not possessed. You're stressed.'

'Well . . .' I stuttered.

'You're telling me you think some sort of dark energy has attached itself to you or the house and is causing all this?'

I picked up my nephew's toy lightsaber from the floor. It went *fzzznct* as I said, 'Honestly, it feels like the house is alive. It's just . . . there's something going on there. Something . . . I don't know, I can't put my finger on it. I just know it's properly getting under my skin.'

The conversation was plunging riskily into 'deep' water. And that's not one of the places we like to go. It's one of the places we like to *not* go. So, Nick surfaced.

'Listen, if you're really worried, maybe get a second opinion. Talk to an electrician, or even . . .' He grinned in an attempt to lighten the mood. 'I don't know, a ghostbuster?'

His scepticism was like a splash of ice water to the face. 'Yeah, maybe,' I smiled. 'Or maybe I'll just sell the bloody place and move into a new-build with no history, no character, and no surprises.'

Nick chuckled again. 'That's the spirit. Don't let a spooky old house get the better of you.'

Then he rakishly slung a kitchen towel over his shoulder and said, 'Isn't it time you let sleeping dogs lie and move on with your life? It's just a house. It's meant to be exciting.'

I knew he was right. I wished that I could just let it lie and move forwards. But, looking back, I don't think that would have stopped what was coming. Nick hadn't seen what I'd seen in the house. He hadn't felt what I'd felt. No. This dog was wide awake and barking for its dinner.

Chapter 11

THE PARAPSYCHOLOGIST

The next morning, I woke up energised. I went down to the kitchen to make tea. As the kettle boiled, I looked out of the window at my ignored garden. I'd barely touched it since moving in and it was by now a no-man's-land of snails, weeds, a sodden barbecue and a few limp plants clinging to life. A neighbour's cat was in the flower-bed, pawing at the soil. Its grey fur was short and slick, with a question-mark tail that wavered above its body like a wisp of smoke. It had gimlet eyes and a pudgy malevolent face. It had the look, to me, of an evil seal.

I sipped my tea and watched it pad about the rose shrub, rubbing its face against the fence, mewing softly. It saw me. Our eyes locked. And then, in a clear fit of the feline fuck-yous, it shuffled backwards and squatted, its hindquarters beginning to quiver. I lunged for the back door. As I fumbled with the key I could see Evil Seal still watching me, straining calmly.

I've always thought of cats as self-conscious creatures – not like dogs, who have no shame or sense of who they are. Evil Seal, on the other hand, knew exactly who it was and what it was doing. When it had finished, it turned around, scuffed soil in the vague direction of its turd, and leapt haughtily over the fence.

As my indignation cooled, I looked again at my garden. The English poet Alfred Austin once said, 'Show me your garden and I shall tell you what you are.'

Well, mine was the neighbourhood cat toilet, and it stank like shit. Something had to be done.

But what? Jason's explanations were comforting in a way. But they had left me with more questions than answers. He'd offered possibilities – Jasmine's anxiety manifesting as poltergeist activity, my own stress creating a place memory. Even a combination of both. Was it just the manifestation of some spiritual energy? Or was there something more tangible, something measurable, that could explain what was happening? I wanted to explore the possibility of scientific explanations. For that, I needed a scientist. I needed a parapsychologist.

—

Contrary to popular belief, parapsychologists are not ghost hunters – though some ghost hunters may claim to be parapsychologists. They tend not to run breathlessly around haunted houses waving 'spirit boxes' and gaussmeters in the air trying to trap the undead. They don't wear boiler suits or push brandy glasses around Ouija boards or search for lost voices in static noise. And crucially, they don't charge you money to cure your sciatica or pass on messages from your dead Granny Gwendoline.

Parapsychology is a branch of psychology dedicated to the study of alleged psychic phenomena.

As in all the sciences, of course there are quacks and hacks, and the mainstream scientific community tends to greet the field with mostly amiable contempt. But the good ones stick like ectoplasm to the principles of scientific inference. That means controlled experiments, appropriate randomisation, masked conditions, barriers to normal information transfer, et cetera. It goes without saying, then, that a serious parapsychologist should debunk far more than they ever evince. Or try to, at least.

'You have to always start from a point of scepticism,' parapsychologist Christine Simmonds-Moore told me via an intermittently shaky video call from America. 'That's why we need psychology to do parapsychology, to rule out normal explanations, which a lot of the time it does. It gets interesting when there are things left over.'

I came across Christine while researching the work of William Roll, one of the founding fathers of modern parapsychology. Roll is among a handful of people credited with dragging parapsychology off the Ouija board and into the lab. There are others, like J. B. Rhine, who chiselled the first notches of credibility and academic rigour into the discipline, but it was Roll who delved deepest into the potential relationship between human consciousness and the physical spaces we inhabit, exploring whether our emotions, memories and actions might leave subtle resonances in the environment.

I wondered if his work might help me. Sadly, there would be no interview with him on this side of the veil because he died in 2012. But a morning on the internet revealed Christine as the next best living thing. She is a British-born professor of Psychology at the University of West Georgia, where Roll spent most of his career, and gave the inaugural Bill Roll memorial lecture, which the university throws each year for parapsychologists from around the world to showcase their work.

Her specialism is, among other things, the psychology of paranormal beliefs, with a particular interest in the role personality plays, and 'clinical approaches to exceptional experiences'. This includes work with the so-called 'God Helmet' – a contraption invented by the legendary neuropsychologist Michael Persinger to study creativity, religious experiences and the effects of stimulating the temporal lobes. It works by sending weak electromagnetic pulses through the skull. In doing so, it has been shown to induce a 'sensed presence' under blinded conditions. Or, more bluntly, it tickles the brain into seeing God. The point? Well, many have taken this as proof that alien sightings, heavenly apparitions, past-life sensations, near-death experiences, awareness of the soul – you name it – are nothing more than synaptic brain fireworks, a mean trick played by our temporal lobes on our prefrontal cortex.

In her findings, however, Simmonds-Moore discovered not that the God Helmet doesn't work exactly, but that it works better on people who already believe in the paranormal. In other words, paranormal beliefs feed paranormal encounters. A believer would say, of course, that this just proves that their brains are simply more attuned to picking up spiritual frequencies.

I tracked Christine down to her office, 4,244 miles across the Atlantic. She was framed by a bruise-purple wall, her straight auburn hair was cut into a fringe as crisp as her British accent, which still had a Home Counties shine despite ten years away from home. The first thing I told her was that 'not believing' has for many years been a core component of *who I think I am*. Though in light of recent events, I confessed, that was beginning to wobble.

I explained my story and she listened silently and patiently, nodding sagely and hmming in all the right places.

When I had finished, she said, 'The first thing to say is that, whatever the explanation, these experiences do happen. And it's true, people often decide ahead of time that it is a ghost, which can lead to psychologically connecting those experiences with paranormal activity and seeing things that aren't there. But what's important to recognise is that, at the end of the day, you clearly had a haunting experience.'

She made air quotes with her fingers when she said the word 'haunting'. And I can't deny that, as she did, a frisson of vindication shot through me. 'My instinct is telling me my brain is making it up,' I said. 'But the more things that happen, the more I'm beginning to wonder if something else might be at play. Something residual from the house's past.'

'Haunted experiences are really complicated and fascinating and I appreciate that you're looking at it with balanced eyes,' she said. 'I get really annoyed when people are like, "Oh it's a ghost. Full stop." Well, what is a ghost, really?'

For Christine, to assign 'ghost status' to what she terms an 'anomalous experience' is, frankly, too easy. 'Psychology can explain a lot of perceived paranormal phenomena, so it's important to systematically investigate each case on its own merits,' she said.

'What about you?' I asked. 'Do you believe in ghosts?'

'I believe in ghost experiences, which can be very real for the people having them,' she swerved. 'I mean, I don't want to say there isn't an afterlife, but I think a lot of experiences can be explained in other ways that can still be parapsychological, without there being intentional spirits trying to communicate with us from beyond the grave. I don't think there is much evidence for that.'

'So, how do you explain experiences like mine?' I asked.

'I am open to more anomalous explanations, but my understanding would lean more towards psi explanations,' she replied.

Psi, in science, is a lukewarm potato. It's not quite as hot as, say, the nature of consciousness or the origin of life. But it's there in the oven of scientific debate, baking slowly on the second shelf.

I had Googled the word before we spoke. It is derived from ψ (psi), the twenty-third letter of the Greek alphabet and the initial letter of the Greek word ψυχή, or psyche, meaning 'mind' or 'soul'. It's the umbrella term for anomalies of the mind that conventional science cannot currently explain. Or, as Christine puts it, 'the anomalous process of information transfer'.

And just because science can't explain it, that doesn't mean it never will. As the American philosopher and psychical researcher William James once said, 'If you wish to upset the law that all crows are black, you mustn't seek to show that no crows are; it is enough if you prove one single crow to be white.'[1]

So far, that white crow has proved an elusive creature. But that hasn't stopped serious parapsychologists from Bill Roll to Christine to dozens of others around the world from trying.

I wanted to know about place memory, and how psi phenomena might help to explain what had happened in my house.

'I think a lot of these experiences can be explained by living minds interacting with other living minds, or information,' she said. 'And maybe information, or emotion, can persist in a physical space.'

Tests have been done on this. It's called psychometry. And Christine has spent a lot of time trying to 'connect information with objects'. In one recent experiment, she and colleagues looked at whether certain people can intuit the difference between identical pieces of jewellery, one that's been worn by another living person and one that's brand new. For this she used rings.

She admitted there are many environmental factors at play here, such as wear and tear, that might influence a subject's decision. But early signs, she said, showed that some people did seem measurably more sensitive to the fact that certain objects had past connections to people, while others didn't. 'We're finding that some people seem able to know which rings might have been worn by a living person compared to matching rings that haven't been worn, particularly those made of silver or quartz.'

William Roll was an early researcher into the idea that people can imprint 'information' onto places or objects that can later be detected by others. He called it 'long body' theory, a phrase he took from Native American lore.

His idea was this: each of us has two bodies. Our 'short body' is the physical self, made of skin and bone, that others can see and touch. But we also have a 'long body' which comprises the innumerable traces we leave on the world around us – the memories, experiences and emotions connected to the objects and places we interact with throughout our lives. This can be as tangible as a worn armchair or a handwritten letter, or as subtle as the scent of pipe tobacco or even the way a room feels to other people after we've left it.

I told Christine that I'd read Roll's 1989 essay 'Memory and the Long Body',[2] where he explains all this. And I got along with most of it, until the bit about atmospheres of rooms.

'I like Bill Roll's idea of the long body,' she told me. 'And while I don't agree with everything he said, I do think it makes some sense.'

She picked up a coffee cup sitting on her desk, then said, 'Think about your favourite mug. It's just a mug to anyone else, but to you, it holds a special meaning. According to Roll's theory, it's part of your long body. Now, if you take a house that somebody has lived in and maybe had intense experiences in, that becomes part of their long body. Roll suggests that places where people have had intense experiences might be more likely to hold these lingering traces. A sensitive person might later pick up on that information, especially if they're going through an intense experience of their own.'

Could it be, I wondered, that a previous occupant's intense experiences left an imprint on this house? Could all this be more than just my imagination? If our long bodies are made up of the traces we leave in the world, could my unease be an echo of the long bodies that were planted here before me? Was Vyas's long body imprinted on these walls we share, separated only by time?

This thought gave me the willies. 'Are you saying there could be some sort of energy, or energetic imprint on the house that's messing with me?' I asked.

'I don't know,' she replied. 'Bill Roll talked about the possibility of zero-point energy, and collaborated with physicists to understand mechanisms that could explain this stuff. He talks about meaning interaction that could have a kind of energetic signature.'

Zero-point energy is the energy that remains when all other energy is removed from a quantum system. It's the silent hum of the universe when nothing else is there, the breath of the void. And it is what many quantum scientists think may explain the underlying fabric of reality itself.

Only, there is a glaring problem with this as a framework for paranormal occurrences – why do they only occur in some places and not in others?' 'Often these experiences are really localised,' she said. 'Even in a house, there are hotspots where things are said to happen. People often report anomalies in certain rooms and not in others. And then it only happens to some people and not others. It might be energetic, but it might not be. I think a better word to use here is information.'

The answer most parapsychologists agree on is that it has something to do with the people involved. Roll's most famous theory, for example, is known as 'recurrent spontaneous psycho-kinesis' (RSPK), which proposes that poltergeists are not caused by disembodied spirits, rather by the unconscious minds of living people, usually those in a state of high anxiety or trauma.

'It might not be the house at all,' said Christine. 'It might be you.'

The conversation was beginning to take a turn down the same shady path I'd shared with Jason Bray.

'Me?'

'Potentially,' she said. 'Think of it this way. You're already in an emotional state from the big changes going on in your life. You're stressed. You are waking up at weird times. Those times are kind of liminal anyway. You're probably sleep-deprived, so you're more labile than you might usually be. You know, those kinds of states can be conducive to weird experiences.'

'So, I turned the radio and shower on with my brain?'

'It's one possibility,' she said. 'I think there's definitely room for some of your experiences being a mind–matter anomaly, maybe influenced by your picking up on information that's already in the space or that you are in a more highly charged state yourself, which we do know relates to mind–matter anomalies.'

Mind–matter interaction, or psychokinesis, is the influence of thoughts, intentions or emotions on physical objects or events. It encompasses a lot of things, from spoon-bending and moving objects from a distance to manifesting positive outcomes and faith healing. It's also, according to some, the direct source of 'poltergeists'.

'Maybe that's a stretch for anyone who's not into psi of the living, maybe they'd say you're pushing it too far, that the only explanation is an entity,' Christine said, making air quotes with her fingers again. 'But I wouldn't jump to the idea of an entity. I think, for you, there are other ways to explain your experiences. The fact that each of the occurrences only happened once, for example, suggests it could be something about this particular period of your life.'

Then she said again, 'It sounds like it's you, like maybe in some way you're having an impact on or interaction with the space.'

My head was spinning. She wasn't finished. 'But there's another important consideration to bear in mind – that these experiences might not all be connected. Some might be genuinely anomalous, but others might just be coincidences. And, in your highly charged state, you could be meaning-seeking.'

'Meaning-seeking?'

I must've sounded confused because she looked at me with a psychiatrist's mix of non-judgemental sympathy and professional concern.

'Yes. Stress is a huge correlate of a range of paranormal experiences, too, both genuinely paranormal ones, and imaginary. Especially when objects start moving about.'

She paused again and smiled. 'I never want to explain people's experiences away. These experiences are highly complicated. And what I normally do is I try and say, "Well, there are all these different possibilities."'

'Like what?'

'Well, first, there could be some anomaly in the house that is causing these things to happen. Second, your psychology is causing them to happen through mind–matter interaction. Or, third, the radio is just one of those things that happen, technical fault or whatever, but it felt weird because you've developed an overarching schema.'

'A schema?' I said, feeling stupider than ever.

'In psychology we talk about Schema theory, which describes the way we organise information into frameworks to help us understand the world around us,' she said. 'So, in this case, even if you don't believe in ghosts, you know the ghost schema, fuelled by all the ghost stories you've heard in your life and the mythology around it. So when things go bump in the night, slugs fall from the ceiling, mice appear, the radio turns on, that's where your mind is conditioned to go.'

She paused. 'But the radio and the doorbell. You're sure there's nothing you can think of that could have caused them to go off?'

'Nothing at all. Unless a mouse scurried over the radio and pushed the on button. But I can't see a mouse with that kind of strength. It's quite firm.'

'Hmmm. I must say that does seem weird. You know, if it does have anything to do with place memory, I know who you should talk to . . . Pamela Heath is a well-respected parapsychologist in California who's still living. She's written a few papers on place memory that I really appreciate, talking about what makes good containers of information, and systems for information. Give her a call. I'm sure she'd talk to you.'

Then she said: 'But I really think the most likely explanation for what you've been through . . . is you.'

Chapter 12

THE PSYCHIC

D r Pamela Heath is a woman of ageless vitality. The only sign that time may have been on her heels was the way she limped from her office chair to retrieve a book from the back of the room. And I think that was a false positive – probably just a horse-riding twinge.

A woman with a hair-trigger laugh reflex, she was an anaesthesiologist until her retirement in 2009, having held various chief-of-department posts in hospitals around America. It was during that time that she found her true calling. Or maybe it found her.

It first happened in the mid-1990s. She'd be on call, at home, waiting for the phone to ring – a nurse telling her someone was going into surgery and she'd have to come in. Some nights it rang, others it didn't. But the strange thing was that, somehow . . . she knew. Vaguely at first, but as she grew more accustomed to the feeling, the stronger it got. Soon, she not only knew that the phone would ring, but also exactly when and what type of case it would be.

'I just knew,' she laughed when we spoke over Zoom. 'It'd be like, "You can stay up as late as you like. You won't get called." And I'm like, "Oh, goody." Or, on other days, it'd be like, "Better get to bed early – you're going to have a 2 a.m. OBG case." And I'm like, "Oh crap!" I go to bed and, at 2 a.m. I get the call. I would wake up always just before the call came in. If there was no call, I didn't wake up.'

'Come on, Pam,' I said, shooting for playful rather than sceptical. 'You're telling me, if you wanted to, you could stay up all night partying on a work night, safe in the knowledge you wouldn't be needed to save a person's life for at least the next twenty-four hours?'

'Well, I wasn't a big partier, but if I'd wanted to, yes.'

'And it worked every time?'

'One hundred per cent of the time. The only time it didn't work was a night when I woke up, the phone didn't ring, and when I asked later if anything had happened, I was told they were going to call, but then the patient died.'

Pam is now a parapsychologist who's written several books and dozens of papers on subjects from psychokinesis to place memory, appeared regularly on American television and given lectures on her work across the USA. She's also a psychic who offers a 'general spiritual cleansing' service for businesses who want rid of unwanted spirits. I told her of my scepticism for that kind of thing, to which she told me it's not everyone's cup of tea – no hard feelings – but assured me that true hauntings are very rare but very real, and her cleansing methods are varied and highly successful. Unlike many ghost hunters, it's not a side of her work she publicises widely, and discretion is her primary USP.

The point of Pam's telephone story was that the unconscious mind wields more influence over our lives than most of us ever perceive. 'It was important to me as a doctor to always be at my best for those patients,' she continued. 'And so, my mind became able to prepare my body for what was coming.'

She let out a jolly laugh. 'And you know what? Since I stopped taking calls as a doctor, I couldn't tell you what was going to happen in the middle of the night. Because it didn't matter to me any more. You see, what people don't realise, it's the unconscious mind that's driving that bus. We might think we're in the driving seat, but we aren't. And when you're under stress, your unconscious looks for creative ways to meet your needs.'

In that moment, my conscious mind was working hard to find a creative way to segue back onto me. But it needn't have bothered; Pam knew. 'Let's talk about you,' she said. 'How can I help?'

I rattled out my story: divorce, house, fires, murderer, slugs, mice, cold spots, shower, doorbell, radio, emotional dip. She listened intently, just as Christine had done, backchannelling throughout with 'hmmms' and 'wows'.

'Very interesting,' she said when I'd finished, looking serious for the first time. 'The house would have awful place memory, then. Just awful.'

'It's worth saying he's not dead,' I said. 'He's alive. In prison.'

'But you'd still have place memory because that's recorded by the living,' she replied.

'He didn't commit any crimes inside the house,' I said, hoping to soften any further incoming blows.

'But you'd still have place memory from just his energy,' she replied. 'How old is your house?'

'About 137 years old.'

'Hmmm.' She let this information filter down for a moment. 'With a place that old, you're going to be having what I would call layered place memory. There will be layer upon layer of place memory, good and bad. Now, where I worry about that with the living is when you have someone like the person you described who is clearly evil, with probably some mental illness stuff going on, they're going to be layering that energy onto objects and everything.'

Then she said, 'But there's something else you must consider before jumping to conclusions. The thing I always say, in cases I run into like this, is: every case is complex. As humans you want to make things simple. You want it to be one thing when it's almost always a little bit of everything, including normal stuff like crosstalk or static electricity triggering electronics or other environmental factors. So, when you approach your data, look at every single incident as separate from the others and see if you can figure it out.'

'Well, the infestations, I guess, I can put down to old houses,' I said. 'Though it makes me uncomfortable that they started happening all at once. The other things, I don't know. I've found no definitive answers.'

'Let's go through it, then,' she said, leaning in. 'The doorbell. Could it be animals? Sometimes I've found it to be rodents chewing on the wires.'

'It's a battery-operated remote plug-in doorbell,' I said.

'Is it high up? I mean, if it's within reach of a dog or even a cat, or fox . . . it can happen.'

I imagined a dog in a flat cap, just out of prison, carrying a box of overpriced tea-towels and rubber gloves, trying his luck at three in the morning. She laughed heartily. 'You just don't know,' she said. 'Plenty of people have Ring doorbell pictures of dogs ringing their doorbells and running off.'

'I think even Scooby Doo would struggle to reach mine,' I said.

'Then it could have been a power surge, or static electricity. Same for the radio.'

'It could,' I said. 'Though it'd have to have been very localised as nothing else in the house played up at the same time.'

'What about the shower?' she said. 'The pipes?'

'That seems the most reasonable answer,' I said. 'The only strange thing is that the plumber checked it and said it was all in good shape. It was a new shower. He'd installed it himself.'

'Old pipes can do funny things.'

I agreed that this felt like the most rational explanation. 'Though the plumber said he'd never heard of pressure causing a shower to run for as long as that,' I added. 'And warm! He'd never heard of that.'

She frowned and blinked, watching me over interlocked fingers. Then she said, 'Something you said about when the radio turned on. What was the song it was playing again?'

'"Mis-Shapes" by Pulp,' I said.

'And you like that song?'

'It's one of my favourites.'

'Oh, that is an interesting detail,' she said ominously. 'You know, the fact it was a song you really like, the timing of it . . . That makes me a little suspicious.'

She again leaned in towards her camera, filling my screen. 'How much do you know about mind–matter interaction?'

As she said this, a fly the size of a sultana buzzed past my ear, drowning out her words. It circled my head, droning in and out of earshot, then alighted on my laptop screen, right on Pamela's nose. Her voice drifted off as I watched it crawl around her face, as if trying to find a way in. As she sat back the fly – for a moment

— became Pam's face, filling her features with its metallic blue body and sinewy wings, like the star of its very own David Cronenberg film. I started and swatted at it with my hand. I missed. Pam flinched. The fly fizzed off the screen and made for the window, which it began head-ramming with frenzied intent. *Even the flies want to get out of this house*, I thought.

'Urgh, I hate those things,' Pamela said, swatting the air around her.

'They seem to be everywhere lately,' I said. 'All over the house.'

'Must be the season,' she replied. 'Now, where were we?'

'Mind–matter interaction.'

'Okay. So . . .' she said, rolling up her mind-sleeves. 'Remember what I said about the power of the unconscious mind?'

'The one that's driving the bus?'

'That's the one,' she said. 'And it will do things that we're unaware of.'

'Like turning on electronics,' I said.

'Maybe. One thing I don't think is emphasised enough in parapsychology is that people think you are either born psychic or you're not. And that's how it is for the rest of your life.'

She shook her head solemnly. 'That is not the truth. A lot of people develop their gift in their thirties and later. It's very common, actually.'

This was hard to swallow. 'So you're saying I may have developed psychic abilities?'

'I'm saying it is possible,' she replied. 'You see, it all ties back to the unconscious mind, and its remarkable capacity to fulfil our needs, even in extraordinary ways. Especially when we're under stress, it seeks creative solutions. And sometimes, those solutions might involve tapping into psychic abilities we didn't even know we had.'

A part of me was quite keen on this idea. I've never really believed in psychic powers. My only experience of them was watching the Israeli-British spoon-bender Uri Geller on GMTV in the 1990s. I still remember the time he claimed to have helped England beat Scotland in Euro '96 by controlling the ball with his thoughts from a helicopter above Wembley. Yet, for the briefest spell, the thought that I might have The Gift gave me a thrill. I saw my own future: roll-neck jumpers, bendy cutlery and lottery jackpots. The fork I'd just eaten lunch with, still on the plate by my laptop, looked momentarily made of gold.

Back on Earth, I sought clarification. 'You mean that my unconscious mind could have turned on the radio, playing a song I love, to comfort me during a difficult time?'

'It's certainly possible,' Pam replied. 'If it were just any random song, I'd be less inclined to think so. But the interesting thing to me is the timing of a song that you really liked. And that would be comforting when you're very stressed. So, to me that suggests there might've been an element of self-soothing by your unconscious, trying to make you feel better.'

'But it didn't make me feel better,' I said. 'It scared the living daylights out of me.'

'Oh, did it?' she said, seeming surprised. 'Well, did it happen again?'

'Not so far.'

'There you go, then,' she laughed joyfully, leaning back in her office chair. 'It didn't cheer you up, so it didn't bother trying it again.'

When she'd stopped laughing, she said, 'I have to say, however, that the fact it did it while you were asleep seems a little illogical. And if it hadn't woken your daughter up then you wouldn't have woken up, so there's no advantage to the soothing quality of it.'

'No . . .'

'Do you follow?'

'I think so . . .'

'Because your unconscious mind is not irrational,' she said. 'It might be twisted and peculiar and it might have a sense of humour that drives you insane, but it has its own logic. It does these things for a reason.'

However far-fetched it might have seemed to me at the time, there was something comforting about the theory that our thoughts independently have our backs. 'We might well have evolved to be aware of environments where bad things have happened,' Pam said. 'I think this is something that would have a real Darwinian survival advantage.'

The idea that our ancestors, navigating a world fraught with danger, developed an intuitive radar for places steeped in fear or sorrow, made a primal kind of sense. It was an evolutionary response to an unpredictable, often hostile, reality. The hairs rising on the back of your neck in a shadowy forest, the inexplicable chill in an empty room, the pervasive sense of unhappiness when you walk into certain homes. Perhaps these aren't just environment-induced illusions – rather, warnings whispered by the past.

But what did this mean for me and my house? Was I merely resonating with the residual energy of a murderer, a man who'd inflicted unimaginable pain and suffering on innocent people? Or was there something more at play, a deeper connection between my own anxieties and a lingering . . . something – energy? information? – that clung to those walls?

'You know who you should speak to?' said Pam, her eyes lighting up. 'Have you heard of Dean Radin?'

I shook my head.

'He's a visionary in our field,' she explained, 'exploring the mind's power to influence the world around us. His work on precognition and mind–matter interaction is groundbreaking.'

She leaned in, a mischievous glint in her eyes. 'He applies principles of quantum physics to even suggest our intentions in the present might shape future events. It's mind-boggling, but he makes it all make sense.'

Pam sat back. 'If anyone can explain the science of how our minds connect with the physical world, it's Dean. Trust me.'

Chapter 13

THE QUANTUM PHYSICIST

Days went by as I waited for Dean Radin to respond to my email. I don't know how many, just that it rained a lot. By then, Lisa, Jasmine and I had settled into a steady routine of child-care. Jasmine started primary school that autumn, around the corner from my house. So, aside from the odd weekend handover, Lisa and I saw very little of each other from then on.

But Jasmine missed her mother terribly and the long, empty evenings were the hardest. To distract her – and perhaps myself – I would read her bedtime stories. Every night, we'd snuggle up on her bed – me, her and her precious Bunny – and read books about ballet-dancing mice, burglars called Bill or bears who lose their hats. It became my favourite time of day.

But there was one story above all else that captured her imagination. Night after night, the same request echoed through the quiet house: 'Daddy, read *The Three Little Pigs*, please?'

I came to despise those lucky little go-getters. Especially the third pig, with his new, secure, normal house that he apparently built without financial backing, not to mention planning permission for a brick house in a primarily wood-and-straw neighbourhood.

Still, Jasmine adored it. And I guess it gave her comfort in a time of upheaval. I'd turn the dog-eared pages, squealing like a pig and growling like a wolf, and her wide blue eyes would drink in every word.

Then, one night, just after I'd closed the book, about to turn out the light, I noticed she looked more thoughtful than usual.

'What's up?' I asked.

She looked at me, a little frown stitched between her eyebrows. 'Daddy,' she said, 'can the big bad wolf blow our house down?'

I am mindful not to over-egg the profundity of this comment. It did, after all, come from a four-year-old more interested in teaching teddies how to cook and eat wooden fruit than philosophical re-readings of ancient fairy tales. But it caught me off guard. I grasped for an answer in the dark.

'No, love,' I side-stepped, stroking a lock of hair away from her face. 'Our house is strong. It's made of love, and love can't be blown down.'

I was smugly pleased with this. But I could see she was thinking it through.

'But whaddabout you and Mummy?' she said. 'Your love got blowed down, didn't it?'

Funny, isn't it, how a four-year-old brain can so simply cut through bullshit and see things for what they really are? This wasn't just our story any more; it was hers too. And she was grappling with it. To most kids, love is like the air they breathe – just there, surrounding them, keeping them safe and happy. Hearts don't break; they just beat. They don't think about love or worry about losing it. It's as natural as a goodnight kiss.

So, when she said that, I was stumped.

I fumbled for words, groping for something age-appropriately meaningful. Something she could hold on to. But my mind was blank. So – without the power of hindsight to guide me – I let slip one of life's most complicated truths.

'Yes, love, but that's different. Sometimes the wolf is inside us.'

—

A wolf *was* inside me. I was sure of that. But what shape it was taking, and how hard it could puff, I wasn't yet sure.

In that time, the words of Christine, Pam and Jason lingered in my consciousness. I spent the next few nights contemplating mind–matter interaction, and the possibility that it all might be me; that my own anxiety could somehow be warping the fabric of my reality. The radio didn't come back on, but the shower did from time to time.

Sleep offered no escape. There were nights when I'd wake, heart pounding, convinced that the doorbell had just rung, only to find the street empty and silent. Except, that is, for the tapping. *Oh god, the tapping!* And the whispering. The bangs. And the footsteps. I still heard them, always at night, plodding through the house, creaking that third step, slamming closed doors. The fire nightmare, too, was by now burning comfortably in my subconscious.

For Jasmine, her room had become her quiet domain, and drawing became her sanctuary. She'd sit at the table or in her room for hours creating little felt-tip worlds: houses under beating suns with flowers and unicorns in the garden. She often drew me and her mother, sometimes together, holding her hand.

One morning, at first light, she came into my room, holding a sheet of white paper. 'I drew you, Daddy,' she said softly.

At the top of the page, in large, somewhat wobbly letters, it declared 'SUPER DADDY'. Below that was me, with big, round ears sticking out of my head, and two black, scraggly circles for eyes that she said were my sunglasses. My arms shot out from my hips, with a chaotic spray of lines for fingers, jutting out in all directions. I seemed to be wearing a cape, which made sense given the title of the work, though it looked more as though I was on fire.

Looming over me was a larger shape, a spiral of heavy, uneven lines that seemed to pull inward. 'What's that?' I asked, pointing.

She looked at it seriously. 'That's your bad emeny.'

'Oh. Who's my bad enemy?'

Her brow tightened around the question. 'Just . . . a bad emeny.'

—

Finally, Radin replied to say he was in the midst of writing his tenth book about the 'science of (real) magic'. But he had time for a video call later that week.

So, we set it up, me in London, and him far, far away in his office in California at the US headquarters of the Institute of Noetic Sciences (IONS), where he is chief scientist.

The IONS is an intriguing place. It was set up in 1973 by Apollo 14 astronaut Dr Edgar Mitchell, after he had a transcendental experience on his way back to Earth. His vision was to build a non-profit organisation devoted to the science of human consciousness and its impact on our lives. 'We are inspired by the power of science to explain phenomena not previously understood,' the institute's website says, 'harnessing the best of the rational mind to make advances that further our knowledge and enhance our human experience.'[1]

The word 'noetic' comes from the Greek word noesis, which refers to the act of thinking or perceiving. And Radin's work ranges from devising experiments to test the possibilities of mind–matter interaction to investigating the potential impact of consciousness on quantum systems.

It is the pinnacle of a career that's seen Radin work pretty much everywhere a parapsychologist can get paid. In the late 1970s, he worked on the US government's top-secret psychic espionage programme, codenamed Stargate. He's been director of the Consciousness Research Lab at the University of Nevada, done stints at the Princeton Engineering Anomalies Research lab and is currently associated distinguished professor at the California Institute of Integral Studies. He's also served as president of the Parapsychological Association five times, written ten books and over 300 scientific articles, and given more than 750 talks across his career. He's also, as it happens, a former concert violinist.

He is, in other words, an extraordinarily interesting man – a man who has dedicated the last forty years to demonstrating that our thoughts *are* things, that our minds *can* interact with reality, and that consciousness is *not* just a passive observer, but an active player in the universe.

—

'It's entirely possible that your mind played a role in those strange occurrences,' he told me off the bat. 'In the laboratory, we've seen evidence that human intention can change physical systems, even at a distance. The effects are not always massively strong, although sometimes they are, but they're measurable. And on the high end, we have phenomena that defy conventional explanation.'

Radin is a slight, bespectacled man with an owlish face and a horseshoe of greying brown hair circumnavigating his head from ear to ear. But perhaps his most striking physical feature is the moustache-goatee that frames his mouth and dances when he talks.

'The point is,' he said, 'we don't have good control over our unconscious. Now, if subconscious fears take root, they could potentially manifest in unexpected ways. And when you add in the possibility of psychic abilities . . . well, all the evidence we have suggests we don't yet fully know what the unconscious is capable of.'

Radin, I imagine, must be devastatingly good in a room. His words roll out of his mouth like carefully vetted pearls, not a duff one among them. His sentences are clear and clean, and after making a point he always pauses, raises both eyebrows and looks at you over his spectacles to make sure you're still on board.

You have to be a good talker when your living spits in the face of conventional thinking. Many mainstream scientists dismiss his findings as flimflam. They accuse him of flirting with pseudoscience, or of squishing together puzzle pieces that don't quite fit. His response to that: nobody has ever completed the jigsaw, and it doesn't come with a box, so who's to say what the picture really looks like? Do we all even see the same picture? Is it even just one picture? As the *New York Times* pointed out in a 1996 interview with Radin, 'they laughed at Galileo, too' when he came up with the idea that the Earth moved round the sun.[2]

Radin chuckled when I mentioned that article; he seemed a little embarrassed. 'The scientific community is just . . . very safe,' he said. 'It's safe because careers depend on going along with the status quo in order to get grants or make tenures. You have to remember, science is a social activity. And like any social activity, it has taboos. And do you know what the most unfortunate aspect of this particular taboo is?'

I did not.

'It is that most scientists will in public, especially in interviews, dismiss it out of hand. But privately, after three beers in a bar, they will start telling you their psychic stories. Everybody has stories that are just . . . strange. And they tell them to me because I am a lightning rod for these sorts of things.'

He shook his head, then said, 'It happens all the time.'

If this is true, I wanted to know what the problem is. Why is science so hesitant to explore ideas that challenge the current scientific worldview, when there is still so much that we don't understand?

Well, for Radin, it is less a question for science than one for philosophy. 'Much of science still operates on a philosophy rooted in classical physics,' he said. 'Quantum mechanics challenges that foundation, and suggests we need to rethink our understanding of reality. The Wigner's Friend experiment, for example, even hints that two people can observe the same thing and see different realities. We need a new framework to make sense of these quantum phenomena.'

—

What I knew about quantum mechanics could've been written on the back of a quark. I knew Schrödinger had a cat who lived and/or died in a box. I knew Heisenberg had a principle. And I knew Einstein famously called entanglement 'spooky action at a distance', where two particles could be linked and, like creepy twins, stay connected even if miles apart. But anything on top of that made my ears hurt and my brain want to escape through my nose.

But then, quantum mechanics – essentially the study of the tiniest bits and pieces that hold the universe together – isn't meant to be fully comprehended. Not yet. Even with its practical applications – from lasers to MRI machines to computers – quantum mechanics remains fundamentally mysterious. It's the puzzle at the core of our existence. As the Nobel-winning quantum physicist Richard Feynman famously quipped in 1964, 'I think I can safely say nobody understands quantum mechanics.'[3]

Things have come along somewhat since then. Still, quantum physicists continue to probe its depths, asking not only, *What are the laws of the quantum world?* but also, *Are there deeper layers of reality that we haven't yet uncovered?*

For Radin, at the heart of it all lies the question of consciousness. If a human being is only made up of a specific set of particles bound together by a few fundamental forces, then: what is consciousness? Is it connected to the quantum realm? Is there some unseen mechanism by which our thoughts can interact with the world we see and touch?

'What I do in the laboratory is ask, "Do mind and matter interact at all, in any way?"' he explained. 'And we have substantial evidence suggesting they do. Not only that, but these interactions aren't necessarily confined to the present moment. Time itself doesn't seem to be a rigid barrier for these phenomena. They appear to transcend our conventional understanding of space and time. So, could we pick up on something like an echo from the past and feel it somehow? I think it's possible. Stranger than that;

empirical evidence suggests our brains can even pick up signals, or influences, from the future.'

Radin's experiments are far-reaching and diverse, from exploring the effects of intention on random number generators to studying precognition and distant healing. But there was one area of Radin's research that has caused a particular stir: his work with the infamous 'double-slit experiment'.

———

To understand the double-slit experiment, you must know a bit about its background. It did, after all, almost single-handedly deliver quantum physics, wet and screaming, into existence.

It was 1801 when a twenty-seven-year-old doctor from Somerset named Thomas Young cut two holes in a piece of paper and held it up to the sun. His plan was to prove Isaac Newton wrong – that light was a wave, not just a stream of particles flying like bullets through the air. It worked and he got famous.

But, held back by the technology of his time, there was one thing he couldn't have known: that this simple test would become one of the most puzzling experiments in modern science. That one day it would challenge everything we understand about the nature of our reality.

Over a century later, scientists tried Young's experiment with particles, the tiniest chunks of matter. They used electrons, expecting them to act like bullets and go through one slit or the other. But they didn't. Instead, they acted just as Young's sunlight had done – like waves. Somehow, it seemed, each electron was going through both slits at once, as if it was in two places at the same time (which physicists now call a 'superposition').

Bewildered, physicists tried to catch the particle in the act. They placed detectors at each slit to see which path it was taking. But the moment they did, its wave function collapsed, and it went back to behaving as they initially expected it to – 'choosing' a single path instead of both. When the physicists turned the detector off again, the quantum weirdness returned. It didn't make any sense.

It was as if the electron somehow knew it was being watched and, like a nude sunbather spotting a neighbour at the window, immediately stopped doing what it was doing and pulled up its shorts.

This is called the Observer Effect – one of the most famously bizarre phenomena in science. Essentially: tiny particles act as though they're in multiple places at once until someone observes them. Simply looking at them, it seems, forces them to 'choose' a position.

—

But what could this mean? Well, it has led some scientists, like Radin, to think that consciousness might be connected to the physical world in a deeper way than meets the eye. It's like reality isn't fully 'set' until someone becomes aware of it.

'Up until quantum mechanics, the idea that the mind could influence matter was considered literally impossible,' Radin told me. 'But with the quantum observer effect, we are gaining increasingly high confidence that when the mind is directed at a physical system, its behaviour changes.'

Now, many scientists say consciousness has nothing to do with this process. They say it's the measuring device itself, the physical interaction with the system, that causes the change in behaviour.

But Radin believes there is more to this story. 'There are ways to detect the existence of a quantum particle without directly interacting with it,' he said. 'This is the realm of interaction-free quantum mechanics.'

He explained a variation of the double-slit experiment where the particle detector destroys its data before anyone has a chance to look at it. 'In that case you don't get a particulate pattern, meaning it didn't change. So, it's not about physical interaction. It's about the knowledge that such a thing *could* happen. The mere possibility of gaining knowledge about a quantum system seems to influence its behaviour.'

—

I could feel my brain inching closer towards my nasal cavity. What Radin seemed to be implying was this: reality is built from the ground up – particles make atoms, which make molecules, which make matter, which ultimately makes us. If these fundamental particles behave in a certain way before we engage with them somehow, we can never directly know what that original state was. It's like hearing the clip-clop of a unicorn down the street, only for it to become a donkey the moment you clap eyes on it. This raises a profound question: is the reality we perceive merely a reflection of our own interactions with the world around us, or is there more to this reality, stuff that exists beyond our perception?

'So, what do you think all this could mean for me?' I asked.

He looked at me as if the answer was dangling by a string off my nose. 'In experiences like yours, I would say in 95 per cent of cases you can find a mundane explanation. But there is always the 5 per cent that doesn't fit. And that, from my perspective, is where it gets interesting. It's either that we haven't done our due diligence properly, or something psychic is going on.'

'The strange things that happened at my house could all have mundane explanations,' I admitted. 'But what gets me is that they've all happened at once. They don't happen regularly. And so far, I have no way of explaining them.'

He thought for a moment. Then he leaned forward slightly, his eyes narrow behind his glasses. 'The thing to remember is that there is so much evidence suggesting subjectivity and objectivity are somehow intertwined. Most things we know about have some sort of memory effect.'

He paused to let the idea sink in. 'If something intensely emotional or even horrific happened in a location, could it change the environment in a subtle way? In principle, yes. How would it be picked up? Well, we don't know.'

His moustache danced merrily to the rhythm of his words. 'We have consciousness, but we don't fully understand its capabilities or limitations. So, could the effects you've experienced be a result of you, acting as a sort of . . . poltergeist agent?'

He raised an eyebrow. 'I'm pretty sceptical about the whole disembodied entity hypothesis.'

'You mean ghosts?'

'Yes, ghosts is one word for it. We know a lot about what living humans can do in the psychic realm, but the evidence for disembodied survival always boils down to what living people report or the effects they can produce. We have no independent way to test if something disembodied is causing it. And yet, poltergeist-like effects happen fairly often, often associated with strong emotions.'

He tapped a finger on his desk. 'In your case, it's difficult to say for sure. If you hadn't known about the house's past, we could establish a baseline and see if the strange occurrences started after you learned about it. That would be your experiment.'

Well, short of uncovering a quantum time loop under my floorboards, or harnessing the non-locality of quantum entanglement to bridge the past and present, we could both see that was not going to happen.

'It's too bad,' he said. 'Then the experiment is confounded. So, we don't know, in your case, was it you or your unconscious that's been doing this?'

'It all points back to the idea that subjectivity and objectivity are somehow intertwined,' he concluded. 'If that's true, then there's the possibility of interaction between mind and matter. And if things can have a sort of "memory effect", could intense emotions or experiences, like the horrific person who lived in your home, leave some kind of subtle trace on the environment? A kind of "echo" that your own unconscious mind might be picking up on and influencing in unexpected ways?'

He looked at me thoughtfully. 'So, could the effects you've experienced be a result of your own unconscious reacting to this echo, or perhaps something else entirely? We can't say for sure, but it's worth exploring.'

'I really don't feel very psychic,' I said.

'Remember what I said at the beginning of our conversation,' he said, almost sympathetically. 'We have good evidence that when the mind is directed at an elementary physical system, its behaviour changes. It may be microscopic in terms of what it's actually doing, but it *is* measurable. So the question then is, does it scale up? Well, all the research that we do suggests that it does scale up. And that is when you have phenomena like this . . .'

He reached under his desk and pulled out a spoon. As he turned it over in his hands it caught the light. It was bent in half – not at the neck like I've seen television illusionists like Uri Geller do, but through the middle of the head.

'. . . I did this myself with a pinch. I was interested in doing this because human fingers cannot do this alone. It takes too much torque. But I did it.'

'How did you do it?' I asked.

'I don't know. I am not particularly sensitive to these sorts of things, not in the way psychics report. And yet I did it. I'd heard so many stories from all sorts of people – some of whom I greatly respected – claiming they'd bent cutlery and other pieces of metal, and it sounded completely ridiculous. So, I went to a spoon-bending party to see for myself, and I did it with only my fingers.'

'And by directing your consciousness onto the spoon?'

'That's right.'

'Could I do it?'

'I don't know. The only way to find out is to try.'

Being 4,000 miles across the Atlantic, I had no independent way of verifying that Radin actually did this. But he had nothing obvious to gain by pretending to bend spoons. He is not a TV magician whose living is to fool paying audiences into believing his mind is special. He is a globally renowned scientist with a reputation built on rigorous empiricism and the principles of scientific inquiry. He is paid to debunk paranormal theories, until he no longer can. He said that he is yet to see evidence that persuades him of the existence of ghosts or the survival of consciousness after death, although the laboratory evidence that the mind can do 'all sorts of interesting things that are lumped under the word "psychic"' is extremely persuasive.

'We're just starting to realise how much we don't know about the universe,' he said. 'There may be countless dark phenomena we can't yet perceive – dark matter, dark energy, dark . . . fill in the blank. Why not dark mind? Quantum mechanics is just the beginning of a new physics, and future breakthroughs could reveal a reality far beyond what we currently imagine.'

Chapter 14

THE PHILOSOPHER

I spent the next three days – mostly at mealtimes – trying to hold dominion over cutlery. I started with a tablespoon, holding it up in a quiet room willing its particles to loosen and its chemical bonds to collapse. I stared at it, focused my thoughts on it, gently rubbed my finger and thumb over it. Nothing. The forks were no more compliant. Even Jasmine's baby spoons held firm. I was beginning to entertain the possibility I might not be psychic after all. In the end, I resolved that if I was psychic, it was not a power I could consciously control.

But, if Dean, Pam and Christine were right, that didn't mean my anxiety-racked subconscious wasn't humming away in the background, firing out little pulses of information, manipulating quantum systems around the house. *Did it?*

If it wasn't my subconscious causing things to happen, what else could it be? Perhaps there was another way to look at this, one I had briefly considered but never fully thought through. One that doesn't need religion, or parapsychology or quantum physics. Simply, chance.

'I think there is a way to explain the weird things that happened to you, and even link them to the bad person who lived in your house many years ago,' Professor Alastair Wilson told me from his home in Oxford. 'But I don't think your answer lies in quantum physics.'

Alastair Wilson is a philosopher of science. He looks just like a philosopher too, with a long, nautical beard to match his long, biblical hair. I've seen Greek statues that don't look unlike him in the V&A Museum, and I'd be surprised if he doesn't have great taste in sandals.

I tracked him down to the University of Leeds, while researching the many-worlds interpretation (MWI) of quantum mechanics – basically the idea that every decision, every quantum event, splits the universe into countless parallel realities, each playing out a different possibility. He's an expert in it. He's also an expert in metaphysics, the philosophy of science and, beguilingly, the philosophy of chance.

It transpired early in our conversation that MWI would be no use to me at all. 'I'm a fairly hard-nosed sceptic about the compatibility of physics with the kind of phenomena I think you have in mind,' he said straight away. 'Yes, there is an entirely respectable approach that takes consciousness to be fundamental to quantum mechanics . . . but I basically don't think there are any distinctively quantum or distinctively physical mechanisms that can link past events directly to the present, except via the usual mediating processes of chemical traces.'

Perhaps he saw me deflate as a physical manifestation of the effect his words had on me, because then he added, 'But that doesn't make what happened to you any less real. And I think to focus all your energies on quantum physics would be to potentially ignore all the fascinating stuff that is going on in the natural world around us, mediated by all sorts of different scientific processes.'

Alastair was sitting at a desk in his four-year-old daughter's bedroom. Behind him was a wall painted in a blue as deep as a midnight sky. On it was a constellation of fluorescent stars stuck randomly about his head. To his right was a window that cast a bright beam of morning sunlight over one side of his face.

'Do you know about the phenomenon of social contagion?' he asked.

'Not much,' I confessed.

'It's a very complex phenomenon where certain behaviours, or even circumstances like yours, become psychologically transmissible. And I would be ready to take seriously the idea of an atmosphere around a house that is created and transmitted, not only socially but also by all the material elements that are in a place there.'

Like Radin, Alastair spoke clearly and carefully. Unlike Radin, he wasn't quick to reply to questions but slow, swilling each thought about his mind until it caught the light. Every time I asked a question, or he was about to start a new thought, he would turn his face up towards the window, allowing the sun to bathe his features. Then, fully charged, he would turn back and launch into words.

'There's a debate in philosophy about whether complex phenomena, like those we experience in everyday life, are truly real,' he mused gently. 'Some argue that only fundamental physics – the basic building blocks of the universe – matters. If that's true, then the idea of past events directly influencing the present, like some kind of invisible wave, seems impossible.'

But this, he said, is too simplistic. 'I don't buy this sort of reductionism because it ignores the richness of the world around us,' he went on. 'Chemistry, biology, psychology – these fields study real phenomena, even if we don't always fully understand how they connect to fundamental physics. We're constantly discovering surprising things about how our bodies, our minds and our social interactions work.'

He tilted his head and blinked wisely. 'Take what you just told me about the things that happened in your house. When you're in a place, there can be a lot going on for you both consciously and subconsciously. I think everyone knows what it's like to walk into a house, or a room, and feel things that aren't quite right. But you can't put your finger on why they're not.'

He was right. There were things I felt those first few weeks I'd moved in. I remembered the sinking feeling I had that I'd made a huge mistake; the clinging, oppressive energy that coloured those early days before the incidents began to occur.

'If I did feel something,' I said, 'I think I pushed it down. Because it was too important to me at the time to make the move a success.'

He nodded. 'Yes, and I'm guessing your neighbours didn't tell you straight away about what they knew about your house?'

'Not straight away, no.'

'Right. So probably, unbeknownst to you, they will have already been behaving differently towards you with that at the back of their minds. There may have been a lot of other things that weren't quite as you would have expected, affecting your subconscious experience, like the way the postman delivers letters or a passer-by peers into your window. So, your whole early experience will have been slightly coloured by that social positioning, and that can have quite a powerful psychological effect.'

I thought back to the strange interaction I'd had with the woman who sold me the house. Her demeanour did seem off, though I couldn't say exactly why. Maybe she just had an awkward energy. Or maybe she was holding something back.

'There is something else to consider,' said Alastair. 'There are some basic facts about the mathematics of chance and coincidence that most people don't fully appreciate.'

He gave his face another light bath, breathed, and turned back to me. 'If you were to roll a die ten times and you got ten sixes, you would find that very surprising, wouldn't you?'

'I definitely would,' I said.

'Right. But if you were to roll a die 10,000 times and at some point in that sequence you rolled ten sixes in a row, you wouldn't find that at all surprising, would you?'

'I guess not.'

'But the mathematical truth is, any sequence within those 10,000 rolls – whether it appears higgledy-piggledy or it is all ones, all twos or even a repeating pattern like one, two, three, four, five, six over and over again – is no more or less likely than any other because of the symmetry of the die.'

I frowned, trying to grasp the relevance to my situation.

'The point is,' he explained, 'in any long series of events, you're bound to encounter some surprising sequences or coincidences. In fact, it's expected. What makes certain patterns seem special is how we perceive them. We tend to find repeating patterns or long streaks more interesting than a jumbled sequence, but mathematically, they're all equally probable.'

Could it really be that simple, *that* soberingly mundane? As if everything I'd experienced in this house was just a random splatter of events, a cosmic Jackson Pollock of happenstance. The bedroom fires, the dry cleaner's assistant who'd become a murderer, the divorce that led me to buy this house, the radio, the doorbell, the shower, the pests . . . all of it, was it all a mere mathematical burp? A roll of the dice in the vast, indifferent universe? And I had spun them up into a scary story?

'We're wired for pattern recognition,' added Alastair. 'It's how we survived. Spotting the tiger in the grass, predicting the changing seasons . . . Those who were good at it, well, they were more likely to pass on their genes.' He chuckled. 'Of course, it can go too far. Seeing faces in clouds, conspiracies in everyday events . . . Our brains are always trying to make sense of our world, even when it doesn't make sense.'

'So,' I said, trying to connect the dots, 'we're primed to see patterns, even when they're not really there?'

'Well, yes and no,' he nodded. 'Sometimes they really are there. It's a delicate balance. We need to be sensitive enough to spot the real tigers, but not so sensitive that we're constantly seeing ghosts.'

He thought again. 'But I think it's important to remember that what you described, those *are* unusual events,' he said. 'Those sorts of things don't happen to people very often. And actually, there's a perfectly high chance that they weren't completely random.'

'What do you mean?' I asked.

'Unusual events leave many, many traces,' he said, 'like ripples spreading out from a stone thrown into a pond. Not just in the house itself, but in the whole neighbourhood, in people's memories.'

He paused, letting the thought dangle in the space between us. 'Think of it this way: before a big event, there's no sign of it. But after, the traces are everywhere. It's like time moves in one direction, leaving evidence in its wake. This is a very obvious thought, of course.'

I didn't want to admit it hadn't been obvious to me at all, so I nodded faux-sagely.

'As these traces scatter all over the place,' he continued, 'they have the potential to interact, like threads weaving together, growing exponentially. When you start with a multitude of different traces, all with the power to interact . . . well, the numbers are astronomical.'

He gestured towards the constellation of star stickers behind his head, as if to illustrate the sheer scale of the possibilities. 'Even if the vast majority of those traces remain unlinked, it only takes a few to connect and become part of a narrative. And these narratives, these connections, they're real things that affect humans in profound ways.'

I thought about that for a moment. 'Are you talking about . . . I mean, the power of expectation is a phrase I've . . .' I trailed off, unsure of where this thought was going.

'Partly,' he said, 'but it's also the complexity of our world. Think about it: a major event leaves so many traces – physical, psychological, social. When those traces align, sometimes in ways we can never track, it can really shake us up.'

He looked out of the window, lost in thought. 'These are real emotions, grounded in real events. It doesn't have to be quantum physics to be real. It's life.'

'Hold on,' I said. 'I don't see how that explains how the radio turned itself on, or the doorbell, or the shower. Are you saying this is all just a random set of events that could have happened to anybody, anywhere, at any time?'

He shook his head.

'That's not what I'm saying. I'm saying the opposite – that the chance of them happening was much higher *because* of the place you were in.'

'Because of the house?' I clarified.

'Exactly,' he nodded. 'Because of the house, its history, the people who lived there before . . . all those traces, all those echoes of the past. Some of them you might be aware of, some you might not. But they all contribute to the likelihood of . . . well, unusual events.'

In that moment, a fly buzzed into earshot, just like one had during my conversation with Pam. Only this time it wasn't alone. There were three of them in the room with me, humming like drones, butting windows and crawling over surfaces. They looked so grotesquely bloated I wondered how they could ever lift off the filth they fed on. It was as if they were looking for something; rotting matter to either lay their eggs in or to liquify and drink. Or maybe they were waiting. I knew there were more downstairs. They'd been growing in number for some time now, with more arriving every day, like an army of mercenaries answering a call.

One of them, now, was sitting on the Escape button of my laptop. It rubbed its bristly face with its forelegs and twitched its prismatic wings with the same haughty insouciance I'd seen in Evil Seal. I waved my hand at it gently so as not to distract Alastair from his point.

'I mean, I'd be surprised if some of the things that spooked you weren't more likely to happen *precisely because* of the situation you were in. Things you might not even realise.'

'Like what?' I asked.

'Well,' he said, 'lots of old houses have dodgy wiring. Maybe a previous owner messed with the electrics, or there are power surges you don't know about. Maybe that's why the radio turned on . . .' He paused. 'I'm not saying that's definitely the reason, but when you consider all the possible factors, all the little quirks of an old house, those strange events become less surprising, don't they?'

Chapter 15

THE SCENT OF A FEELING

One sunny day, a long time ago, a fly flapped its wings in the bedroom of a house. The vibrations of those wings sent minuscule pressure waves rippling through the air, creating a buzzing sound. This irritated the highly strung homeowner and she swatted the fly dead. But, in doing so, she knocked an antique vase off the windowsill. The vase shattered, and a sharp fragment of ceramic lodged itself under a floorboard.

That little shard lay there unnoticed for the next fifteen years, wedged between the wooden board and a loose nail holding it in place. But constant footfall on the board caused the shard to shift closer to the nail. Slowly, it loosened. Then, one cold, dark night, the now-elderly woman snagged her toe on the board, tripped and fell. She hit her head on the dresser and died.

This woman lived alone and had no children, so the house went up for auction. As chance would have it, a local landlord was at that auction, looking to expand his portfolio. He bought it cheap. More interested in turning profits than proper maintenance, he would rent it to a family. They in turn, seeking to ease their own financial difficulties, sublet the bedroom to a young man recently arrived from India. The landlord never fixed that loose floorboard.

So, one evening, the young man – burdened by loneliness and homesickness – paced restlessly in his room. With every tread of his foot, that floorboard squeaked. And eventually, after fifteen years in that spot, the shard of ceramic finally wiggled loose and pierced a wire running beneath the floor. The exposed wire sparked, catching a nearby rug. The bedroom was quickly engulfed in flames.

The fire engines, the sirens, the flashing lights – they ignited something dark within the young man. Perhaps he later made a string of hoax 999 calls, craving the chaos and attention. But the thrill faded, and he sought a new, more sinister kind of power: vulnerable women walking alone at night. His crimes escalated until he was finally apprehended and imprisoned.

Across the next fifteen years, the house changed hands a few times before a freshly divorced father moved in. He was oblivious to the house's past. But the house remembered.

The fires had ravaged the house's wiring, which the former landlord, cutting corners wherever possible, had paid his unqualified cousin to repair. And so, one February night at 5.23 a.m., a surge of electricity, delivered by the chaotic tangle of wires haphazardly spliced together inside the fuse box, pulsed through the house. And there . . . in the quiet of the night, the radio crackled to life.

I may never know the truth.

But it is not a test to imagine the past reaching out, through years and walls, to touch the present. Maybe Alastair was right: my radio, the shower, the doorbell *were* the culmination of countless tiny events, a butterfly effect of misfortune and neglect stretching back decades.

Or maybe we did it all with our minds. Either way, none of it explained what the house seemed to be doing to my health.

—

I came back from my birthday weekend away with Jody refreshed. Ramsgate's salty air and cries of gulls had been a merciful change from the gloom that had settled over me since buying the house. The sickness I'd been feeling, all the anger and sadness and foggy lassitude, had lifted. And in its place had come a lightness and clarity of thought that I hadn't felt in months. Frankly, it was a wonder Jody had stuck around this long.

Maybe things at home aren't so bad, I thought as I travelled back from King's Cross on the Victoria line. *Maybe everything I've been feeling is just a long hangover from divorce, and this holiday is the spiritual paracetamol and bacon sandwich my body needed.*

The light was dwindling by the time I got home. The house was still there, its white facade reaching out through the gloaming like a tormented ghost. I stood for a moment on the pavement outside, key in hand, and looked it up and down. The plastic door, the grubby window frames, the flaking render. It looked sad in the deepening twilight, almost pitiful.

Okay, deep breath, I thought. *You're just a house. Walls and floors. Windows and doors. Just a house. We're still getting to know each other, aren't we? Maybe that's all this is. We just need time. Time to settle, time to understand each other. Yes. That's it. Just time.*

I turned my eyes up to the house again and, for a split-second, I felt it look back.

Something was different. When I pushed open the front door a sudden wave of nausea crashed over me. A sickeningly sweet stench permeated the air, like rotting fruit mixed with something . . . unnameable.

I'd battled smells here before, but this wasn't damp or drains. I suddenly wished Jody hadn't had the work meeting that meant she'd returned to her flat. That familiar sense of dread was returning. And with it, the taste of death oozing down the back of my throat.

I dropped my bag by the door and moved cautiously through the downstairs rooms. My nose was leading the way. The smell was strongest in the hallway. It was a suffocating presence that made my stomach churn. I felt the sudden urge to vomit but gulped it back down and moved into the living room. There, it seemed to fade, replaced by a faint whiff of decay coming from the fireplace.

I knelt down and shone my phone's torch up the chimney. Nothing but soot and cobwebs. A pigeon's feather floated out. Immediately, the smell of decay vanished, chased away by a musty sweetness wafting from the kitchen. It was beginning to feel like a sinister game of hide-and-seek – or hide-and-sniff – as the stench shifted and swirled around me. Like the tapping sounds I'd heard a few weeks before, it was moving about.

I rallied and checked the kitchen meticulously. I opened cupboards, peered under the sink and even emptied the bins. Nothing. It felt as if the house was mocking me.

Exhausted and frustrated, I sprayed half a can of Oust I found under the sink and collapsed onto the sofa. Was that tapping I could hear? *Was it back?*

I glanced at my phone; the urge to call Jody was overwhelming. But what could I say? 'Happy birthday to me, my house smells like death and I think I'm going mad'? She already thought I was being paranoid. This would only make her worry.

No, I had to deal with this myself. I had to find the source of this phantom stink. I stood up, determined not to be defeated by a smell. I would tear this house apart if I had to. But I would find it. Then again, I was tired from travelling and, suddenly, even more depressed. And as Benjamin Franklin should have said, *why do today what can be put off until tomorrow?* I went upstairs – as far away from the smell as the house would permit. I climbed into bed.

The next morning, I came downstairs in my dressing gown and steeled myself for another assault on the nostrils. I gripped the living-room door handle, held my breath, and went in.

The smell was gone. Nothing. Just the faintest hint of dusty air and the ghost of lavender air freshener. The relief was gorgeous. I took a deep, greedy breath of this blessedly clean air. Maybe I had imagined it. Or dreamed it? But it had smelled so real, so awful.

'The mind is a powerful thing and potentially stress and anxiety could have an effect on creating olfactory hallucinations,' Professor Carl Philpott later told me from his office at the University of East Anglia.

Carl is a renowned ear, nose and throat surgeon and rhinologist who specialises in smell and taste disorders. In fact, there is a word for when people imagine smells that aren't there: phantosmia. It is a condition that has been linked to several illnesses, from Covid-19 to head injuries to some types of dementia. But studies have also uncovered an overlap between olfactory dysfunction and depression. However, Carl said the causal relationship is unclear

— something of a 'chicken and egg' situation. 'On the one hand, there is evidence that people with depression have smaller olfactory bulbs, which are the relay stations for the smell nerves,' he told me. 'But equally, people who experience smell loss or distortions report higher rates of depression and anxiety. So, which comes first? It might be a bit of both.'

Grief, for example, is a common trigger of phantosmia, and people in grief often report picking up a lost loved one's scent after their death — their favourite perfume, the whiff of cigar, a leather jacket.

'You know, high states of anxiety can result in all sorts of physical and neurological symptoms,' he concluded. 'There's no reason the sense of smell should be any different.'

—

Well, I hadn't imagined it. Because a week later it returned. My youngest brother, Spike, had come over to see the house and help me to paint the hallway. He's severely colour-blind, an ocular deficiency for which I'm convinced nature compensated him in the nose. He thought he knew what the scent was.

'It smells like dead things,' he said as he paced about the living room, nose first like an airport sniffer dog.

'Dead things?'

'Dead things. It can't be mice, unless you've got a mouse graveyard down there. They're too small to make that smell. If it's a dead animal, it must be bigger. A dead rat under the floorboards? A fox? A neighbour's cat?'

Haven't seen Evil Seal in a while, I pondered, privately. Then I steadied. *He'd be too fat to squeeze under the house anyway.*

I was impressed with Spike. He had a deeper knowledge of dead animals than I'd ever given him credit for. I suppose a lifetime of not being listened to tends to give youngest siblings a secret power – the power to discreetly store up knowledge and unleash it when family members least expect it.

'I had a family of rats living under the shed at the end of my garden at art school,' he said, casually. 'The exterminator said the only way to get rid of them was to lay poison and wait for them to die.'

He let out a learned breath. 'It was horrific. Dead rats all over the garden, in bushes, behind pots. Rats the size of small cats, rats the size of rats, baby rats. We didn't feel good about it. And I'll never forget that smell. Never.'

He shuddered. 'This is a bit triggering, to be honest.'

'Why does it keep coming and going, then?' I asked.

'Does it?'

'Yeah. And I've not been able to locate a source. Honestly, it's like the house itself is rotting from the inside out.'

We spent the next hour hunting for the source of the smell, just as I had after Ramsgate. But we found nothing. Fortunately, the fresh paint we slathered across the hallway drowned out the death odours. By the time it had dried they'd vanished again.

Over the next few days, I considered the options. I was sure the smells I was chasing were not literally wafting up from the past. That *did* sound crazy. Something had to be causing them; I just didn't know what. But what if, all this time, I'd been inhaling something else as well? Some sort of . . . physical residue from the past.

Can a house soak up 'vibes', like cigarette smoke in wallpaper? Can feelings hang around in a physical environment long after the residents have left, their laughter or their sorrow somehow embedded in the walls? The science of this phenomenon is the study of 'emotional residue' – which explores the possibility that our feelings leave invisible traces, imprinting themselves on the spaces we inhabit. It's the theory that emotions might have a physicality; a presence that lingers after the source has departed. Even Alastair agreed that we've all walked into a room and felt an immediate shift in atmosphere – that ineffable sense of unease that seems to hang about some houses. Perhaps it's an old hospital ward, a former prison cell, or even just a house with a history of sadness or conflict.

Increasingly, researchers are finding evidence that this might not be as far-fetched as it sounds. Scientists have even proved that our bodies constantly pump out invisible chemical 'messages' that other people detect and physically respond to, not only in the moment but even after the source has gone.

What if Vyas had left something here, if not a psychic energy, then something more tangible – a kind of olfactory ghost that was influencing me physiologically?

—

Jody has a friend called Laura who lived in a notorious property from the age of thirteen. Her parents moved with her and her two sisters into the large Georgian house in the Kent countryside in the mid-1990s.

'It was a big house, quite old, with a gnarled old tree in the garden that we called the hangman's tree,' she told me one evening over dinner. It was the cellar of the house that really made her skin crawl. 'It had a weird smell,' she said, 'and just a really creepy, unhappy vibe to it.'

It didn't take long for the family to discover what had happened down there in the darkness some twenty years earlier. 'My parents bought the house from an old man, a widower,' she said. 'Local rumour had it that he was abusive and used to lock his wife in the cellar, sometimes for days on end. Then, one day, she hanged herself down there.'

It wasn't just the knowledge of her new home's history that freaked out Laura either. 'There was one room on the ground floor – we called it the breakfast room, but we didn't use it much. I think the previous owners used it a lot though.'

She took a sip of wine. 'That room especially, it always had a sort of weird, lingering foreign smell,' she recalled. 'It's very hard to explain, but it was an old smell.' She paused to collect her words. 'It just smelt like *other* people.'

The family had dogs, so they were used to bad smells in the house. It wasn't that. 'The smell would lessen as we lived in the house, but when we went away, no matter what we did, it would always be back when we returned.'

Then one day, while Laura and her sisters were playing hide-and-seek in the house's attic, they pulled open an old cupboard to find a dress, hanging. 'It was a lilac dress, old-fashioned, like something Dusty Springfield might have worn,' recalled Laura. 'It was dusty but in perfect condition, just frozen in time. And you know what? To me, it had the exact same smell as the room downstairs – old, foreign. It was *her* smell.'

Laura added, 'While we had a very happy childhood there, I

think you could feel the sadness in some of those rooms – a really oppressive, Miss Haversham feel.'

Then she said, 'It was almost as if the past hadn't truly . . . you know, passed. It was like that couple's sadness somehow stayed behind in parts of the house long after they themselves had gone.'

Chapter 16

THE SMELL SCIENTIST

The Irish poet and Nobel laureate W. B. Yeats was an out-and-proud believer in the paranormal. Ghosts, he thought, could be as vivid as words. Only, when his friend and fellow Irish poet Louis MacNeice asked him if he'd ever actually seen one, he demurred coyly, 'Oh no.'

Then he rallied, and said, 'But I have often smelt them.'[1]

Yeats would later expound in detail his experiences of sniffing out ghosts.[2] 'Sweet smells were the most constant phenomena,' he wrote, 'now that of incense, now that of violets or roses or some other flower, and as perceptible to some half dozen of our friends as to ourselves, though upon one occasion when my wife smelt hyacinth a friend smelt eau-de-cologne.'

As for bad smells, he claimed they served as omens. 'A smell of cat's excrement announced something that had to be expelled,' he wrote; 'the smell of an extinguished candle that the communicators were starved.'

The aroma of burned feathers, he reckoned, heralded a coming illness to the family. 'I can discover no apparent difference between a natural smell and a supernatural smell,' he concluded, 'except that the natural smell comes and goes gradually while the other is suddenly there and then as suddenly gone.'

—

I don't believe that a spirit of any kind was behind the smell in my home. I only knew that it stank, and I didn't know why.

'People don't like the notion, but when it comes to communicating with each other through smell, we are basically big, glorified rats,' Israeli neurobiologist Noam Sobel told me from his office at the Weizmann Institute of Science in Rehovot, Israel. 'We are constantly releasing chemicals into the air around us that produce both hormonal and behavioural changes in other humans. And most of us have no idea how much this can affect us.'

Professor Sobel is one of the world's most influential smell scientists. As head of the institute's Department of Brain Sciences, he spends his days unlocking the secrets of smell, revealing its profound influence on our brains and behaviour.

Sobel's findings are remarkable: he's shown that when we meet someone, we unconsciously 'sniff' the 'chemical cloud' that surrounds each of us – a unique vapour of hormones, bacteria, fungi, yeast and trillions of other molecular traces – that steers how we feel and whom we trust. He and his team have even developed 'electronic noses' that measure those molecules our bodies emit, and a wheelchair controlled simply by sniffing.

The scientific word for communicating through smell is 'chemosignalling'. Chemosignals are not controversial like pheromones, but they are poorly understood, and scientists have only identified a handful. Still, scientists such as Sobel are constantly uncovering new ways we use chemosignals to speak silently to each other, from falling in love to recognising danger – the whole gamut of human emotion.

Sobel and his team, for example, have discovered a molecule in women's tears that, when sniffed, lowers aggression in men by 43.7 per cent.[3] More intriguing, they have isolated a similar molecule released by babies' heads that, when smelled, increases aggression in women, but blunts it in men.[4] 'It's called hexadecanal,' he explained, 'and it makes evolutionary sense because, in the mammal world, males can be a danger to their young and sometimes even kill their own offspring. Females, on the other hand, are biologically wired to protect their babies at any cost.'

In another striking experiment, Sobel took 'fear sweat' from a group of skydivers and asked people on the ground to sniff it under controlled conditions.[5] Overwhelmingly, they reacted with increased electrical conductivity in their skin – a classic fear response. In other words, humans, like many other mammals, can literally smell fear.

As Sobel says: 'That thing on your face is not there for nothing . . . It's a very, very good detector. And you use it, like all mammals, in all sorts of complex ways.'

Sobel has a strong face. His features looked as if they were chiselled out of his head by a sculptor with great talent, but on a tight deadline. His grey hair was shaved close to the scalp, leaving little to distract from his nose, which is a good size – the perfect tool for a man of his profession, you'd think. Only, he'll be the first to tell you a strong nose doesn't necessarily equate to a strong sense of smell. That's all done in the brain.

With all this talk of people's scent, I couldn't help wondering what Sobel smelled like. I imagined it was a mixture of something pleasantly musky and hand sanitiser, infused with a subliminal tinge of whatever chemosignal we emit when we're excited. Because Sobel grows infectiously animated on the subject of smell.

'There are particular odorants that we can detect in parts per trillion,' he said, leaning in towards his camera so his face filled my screen. 'That's insane. I mean, we've identified a particular molecule that we believe is a potential social chemosignal that, if I were to drop a single pipet of it into an Olympic swimming pool, you could smell the difference between that, and a pool without it.'

'Me?' I said.

'Any human with a properly functioning olfactory system,' he said. 'That's how good at smelling certain molecules we are.'

As he said this, I felt a sudden itch at the end of my nose. He was now explaining how androstadienone and estratetraenol, two steroids found in human sweat and saliva, are believed to be the invisible puppeteers of our socio-sexual interactions, subtly shaping our perceptions of attractiveness and trust. Listening, I scratched the underside of my nose with the knuckle of my index finger. Then I placed my hand over my mouth, before stroking my chin. I didn't know I was doing this at the time; I only know now because, at that moment, Sobel pounced.

'Right there,' he said, lurching forward. 'You see? I just noticed it.'

'Noticed what?'

'You were just sniffing your fingers so carefully.'

'Was I?' I said, taken aback.

'You did it without even thinking,' he said. 'We all do. But because I measure that behaviour in humans, I cannot unsee it now. Just like dogs, we're constantly sniffing ourselves, and each other, we're just not trained at noticing it.'

I found the thought of this unsettling – that below the surface of our conversations and conscious gestures lies a silent world of smelly tells and unspoken coercions, whose biological mechanisms nobody truly understands.

'Think about hugging,' he went on. 'You put your arms around someone, and you inhale them. It's built-in behaviour. We're constantly sampling each other's body odour, and our own by way of comparison, because it has a very powerful effect on how we interact with each other, how we choose partners and friends, whether we form an instant connection with someone or not.'

I wanted to know about emotional residue. Is it real? Are the chemosignals our bodies send into the world not only detectable in the moment, but even after we're gone? Could Vyas have left his own bodily traces in my house that I was somehow picking up? 'I'm not suggesting that the awful smells in my home are Vyas, whatever they are,' I said. 'But could he, or someone else from the past, have left a cocktail of chemosignals that are inducing some kind of fear response in me, now?'

'This raises a very interesting question,' said Sobel. 'First of all, yes. I totally buy the idea that chemosignal molecules can linger in an environment after the person has left for a limited time – maybe even a few days. I would even be prepared to build an experiment around that. But for ten years?'

He shook his head. 'I wouldn't waste my time on that experiment.'

'So you're saying that unless a house has been hermetically sealed for a decade, like an exhibit in a museum, any emotional residue or chemosignals would be too diluted to detect?' I asked.

'In theory, yes,' he said. 'But look, I'm the last scientist you'll find who says we understand everything. We don't. So it could be that there's a model for lingering emotions for ten years as well. It's just that I don't know it.'

'So, in your expert opinion,' I posed in as lawyerly a tone as I could muster, 'it's not completely impossible that a person could leave traces of themselves in a place that could affect people ten years down the line?'

He smiled sportingly. 'I'm not saying it's impossible, no. I'm just saying I don't have a chemosignalling model to explain it. I do have a model that can explain it for a limited time. I'll even say I buy it at the most intuitive level across a longer timeframe.'

He was nodding as he spoke. 'I totally buy it. I just don't have an explanation for it.'

I thought perhaps I'd caught a scent of my own here. So, I followed it. 'Could a house, say, absorb emotions into, maybe . . . its wallpaper, like cigarette smoke, or mould?'

The smile abandoned his face as he pondered this for a moment. 'You know,' he opened, tilting his head. 'You've given an idea for how it could last longer than I'm proposing. It's funny, because my lab is made for olfaction experiments, with HEPA carbon filtration to control the airflow and specially treated walls so they cannot absorb anything. So, it's a completely unnatural setting.'

He paused again for thought. 'I'm not used to thinking of a natural environment in this respect. So, if you have some sort of agent in the walls that's doing an absorption and slow release, like the wallpaper you just brought into the game, well . . . who knows? You might have something there.'

Sobel leaned back in his chair, considering the possibilities. 'If you would've tasked me as an engineer with inventing some sort of wallpaper that will absorb the odour and release it slowly over time? That's probably doable. So yeah, maybe you have your long-term model there as well.'

———

In the days since Spike helped me paint the hall, the smell had grown stronger, coming and going like a polluted offshore breeze. But its origin remained maddeningly elusive. By now, it had taken on a distinctly feral character: a mix of rotten bins with something sweet. When it peaked, it seemed to come out of the walls themselves, like gusty breaths from a monster living in some old forgotten cavity of the house.

I wanted a second opinion. So I emailed the world's other foremost smell neuroscientist – the magnificently named Jasper de Groot. His specialism was the smell of fear.

'We know that when people are exposed to the odour of someone in a fearful state, they show signs of fear themselves, even if they have no other information about the situation,' he told me. 'We have an incredibly acute sense of it, even at the very lowest thresholds.'

He has even found that fear sweat contains a peculiar molecular cocktail that's not found in any other emotional emission. They just haven't yet worked out what exactly it does once inside a person's nose.

For de Groot, smell is our 'magic' sense. Of course, he would say that. 'The magic of odours lies in their invisibility,' he told me. 'You're being influenced by something you cannot see.'

In de Groot's mind, what makes smells more magical than, say, sights or sounds is precisely that: their capacity to linger in an environment after the 'sender' has already left. Like Sobel, he wouldn't stake his reputation on the notion that chemosignals hang about for years, but he wouldn't dismiss it either. 'What can be supported by scientific fact is that people can "catch" emotions just from smelling someone's scent – whether it's fear, happiness or even intense joy,' he explained. 'There's also evidence that these emotions can linger . . .'

He went on, 'We often sample the emotion of a person on an absorbent compress and then we put that in the freezer for a couple of months and when we defrost it the effects are the same. We also know heavier, sticky compounds, like tobacco smoke, vanillin and certain fatty acids can adhere to fabrics and other absorbent surfaces and be smelled much later.'

I asked if he could apply the same principles to, say, a house, assuming there are similarly absorbent surfaces or materials that could potentially collect human molecules. 'There are, of course, many more variables here, so we are moving rather into unknown territory,' he replied. 'When it comes to chemosignalling, we don't have the data on that yet.'

'So it's impossible to say?' I pushed.

He sat quietly for a moment, then he said, 'According to our current understanding, yes. But hypothetically, I would say that it is not completely unlikely at all.'

Chapter 17

THE MALEVOLENT MANOR

Since all this began, I found myself spending more time in the British Library in London's King's Cross, which is nothing like the grand, cloistered cathedral of knowledge the name implies. From the outside, it looks more like a giant, windowless municipal leisure centre, or minor-city polytechnic. All red bricks and sharp angles – the telephone directory of buildings.

But it's warm on the inside, full of life and learning, from students who go to flirt in dark corners to dusty academics lingering over ancient texts. I went there to work in the days when I didn't have to do the school run. I went partly for the free Wi-Fi, but mostly to escape. My mind felt lighter there, not gunky and congealed like when I was at home.

One afternoon, while trying to find a copy of William Roll's 1973 book *Poltergeists* (which, incidentally, had mysteriously vanished from the vault), I bumped into an old acquaintance called Jessica. We went for a coffee, and she told me about the new flat she and her boyfriend had just moved into in Kentish Town.

'Did you burn sage to cleanse it?' I joked, not expecting a serious answer.

She looked at me blankly over her tortoiseshell glasses.

'Of course,' she said as if the answer was so obvious I might as well have asked if she'd remembered to flush the loo on her last trip.

Then came the inevitable question – the one I'd come to both dread and darkly relish. It was a conversational landmine, but also a spark. 'I haven't seen you since you moved house. How is it?'

Every time this question came, I'd tell the story with a carefully calibrated blend of nonchalance and intrigue. And then, something always happened. Necks craned, eyes widened, mouths formed silent 'O's. The room, no matter how crowded or noisy, seemed to tilt towards me. It was like casting a spell.

Everyone, it turns out, has a morbid fascination with the macabre. Even the die-hard sceptics, after they'd scoffed and arched their eyebrows, couldn't hide the hint of thrill that lined their disbelief. It was just as Dean Radin had said about physicists. And then – and this always happened – the floodgates opened.

Stories tumbled out – shadowy figures sitting at the ends of beds, inexplicable bumps in the night, that one creepy house everyone knew growing up. It was a ghoulish chemistry of shared experience. Suddenly, we were connected, bound by a mutual intrigue over the secrets houses keep, and how little we know about their mysteries.

Jessica had a story. It was about a woman whose house had a terrible past. 'Oh my god,' she said. 'You must speak to Natalie up in the Wirral. Her story has so much in common with yours. Strange things happening at night, a dark past. If you don't find answers, you may at least find peace of mind that you're not alone.'

As chance would have it, I have family in that part of England's north-west. So, one late-autumn weekend, I paid her a visit.

—

Natalie's home was not at all like mine. For a start it was gorgeously grand. Built in the 1850s by a local landowner, it has twenty-one rooms, set in seventeen acres of Wirral countryside. A long, winding gravel driveway leads up to a bright red door, past green lawns and tall trees that lead off into a great wood beyond the property's boundary. It has an orchard, a converted stable, walled flower gardens and a conservatory that looks out onto a man-made fishing pond with a jetty. The moment they first pulled up outside, Natalie knew. 'It was my dream home,' she told me. 'Our forever home. I just knew that we would be happy here and give the kids the childhood we never had.'

It was a bright afternoon on the day I visited, and what I saw inside was far from the sinister old fright factory I'd been led to imagine. Natalie had painted every room a different bright colour – her office was jungle green, her son's room was Evertonian blue, her daughter's room was gold, and the kitchen was deep crimson and white. If a house were ever a reflection of its owner's personality it was this. Natalie, a children's author who also runs a youth literacy charity, was effervescent. 'Don't get me wrong,' she said as she floated through the stone courtyard at the back of the house. 'In the daytime, this is a beautiful place.'

It wasn't, she said, until dusk that things began to get weird. She'd be in the kitchen and see a movement out of the corner of her eye, feel a light gust sweep across her back, or a sudden temperature change in the room. 'I'd turn around, but no one was ever there,' she said, making us a cup of tea. 'Just as the darkness was beginning to settle. Just then, the place takes on a completely different feel. You could always hear whisperings and get the sense of not being completely alone.'

Other people felt it too, she said. 'Even people who are not the sort to mention atmospheres of places would say in the daytime, "Oh, isn't this lovely and light?" And when it got dark they would say, "Oh, this is a bizarre place."'

A few months into life in their new home, her son Nate, then four, began to suffer nightmares and bouts of sleepwalking. 'He kept talking about a bear he'd see in his dreams,' she said. 'He was convinced it lived in his room.'

They put it all down to a four-year-old's overactive imagination. He'd soon grow out of it, they thought.

—

It was a cold night in 2017 when Natalie and her husband were awoken by a piercing scream. Nate. It could only be him. Natalie threw off her bed covers and rushed towards her son's bedroom. But she stopped short on the landing. Bathed in a cold beam of moonlight, Nate stood silhouetted against the window, facing away from her. He wasn't screaming any more. He was frozen, staring down the stairs, with his arms outstretched like a starfish. For a split-second Natalie stopped and she could feel the bitter air on her face as she strained her eyes, alert, freezing, confused.

Nate? Nate? Are you okay? Nate?

She was saying his name, but he didn't respond. He didn't move. He didn't even seem to hear her. At that moment Liz, the nanny, materialised on the stairs. Closer to him, she rushed forward, hands outstretched to soothe. That's when he spoke. He spoke, and it was *him*, but it wasn't his voice.

'It was a voice I'd never heard him use before, not like a machine or a ghost from a movie,' Natalie said. 'The words came out of *his* mouth, but they were completely flat, devoid of any emotion.'

I don't want you. I don't want you.

Natalie's heart was racing. She was drained and frightened and shaking and she could see her breath in the cold air. She scooped him up and carried him back into his bedroom. A pale light wisped in through the crack in Nate's curtains, making the corners of the room it couldn't reach seem fathomlessly dark. 'I flicked the light switch, but it didn't turn on,' she said. 'Nate was hot, so I gave him a drink of water to cool down.'

She sat in the armchair she'd once used to nurse him as a baby and held him tightly against her body. She could feel the heat radiating out of him, and his heart beating against her chest, and there was also the smell. It was the smell of burning, but nothing was on fire.

Shhhh, it's okay, she tried to comfort her son. But he wasn't calming. He was looking over her shoulder into the corner of the room with open, frightened eyes. Then he raised his right arm. He raised it slowly and mechanically and then he pointed.

Mummy, I don't like the way he's looking at me.

Those words still haunt Natalie today. But it was what happened next that terrified her most. 'I didn't want to look, but my eyes were being drawn to that corner,' she said. 'It was so dark . . . so, so dark. And I couldn't see anything there.'

She was peering into the corner of the room, straining her eyes until they hurt. *There's nothing there*, she told herself desperately as she fought the urge to shut her eyes and pray for help. *There's nothing there. There's nothing there.*

Then she heard it. From the black corner came a noise. It was a noise that under any other circumstances she might've dismissed as a gust of wind outside, or a draft caught in a chimney. But it wasn't the wind; it was inside the room. There was no mistaking it. 'It was just . . . a long, drawn-out exhalation of breath,' she said. 'There's no other way I can describe it.'

Then, silence.

Tears of fear running down her cheeks, Natalie picked Nate up again, and went back into her bedroom, where her husband was now awake.

'I was trying to tell him what had happened, trying to get my words out,' she said. 'But it must've sounded so garbled. He thought I was half asleep and my mind was playing tricks.'

No, she whispered. *Something's going on in that room. I'm not putting him back in there.*

She collected her daughter and – together with the nanny – they slept on sofas in the living room. 'All through the night there were knocks, rumbles, the lights flickered, there was this horrible charged energy,' she said. 'And the smell . . .'

'What was the smell like?' I asked, a question in which I now had a particular interest.

'It's hard to describe,' she said. 'It was kind of like burning electrics, and later in the night it changed and smelled sweeter, almost like incense.'

'What did your husband think of it all?' I wanted to know.

She rolled her eyes and smiled in a 'what's-he-like' kind of way. 'He's very logical and always looks for the most practical explanation,' she said. 'He reasoned that we all had to be half asleep and imagined it.'

But Natalie knows she didn't imagine it. Nor did Liz the nanny, who handed in her notice the next day and moved back to the city two weeks later.

'We've been through quite a few nannies over the years,' said Natalie. 'The house tends to scare them off.'

Other things have happened too. When her children were younger, the baby monitor would often pick up their little voices talking to something that wasn't there. On other occasions, the soft sound of singing would crackle through the speaker. 'More than once a nanny would think I was in there with the kids and bring me a cup of tea, only to find the room completely empty,' she said.

Then there was the time Natalie awoke to see Nate standing at the end of her bed. 'He had this white light shining across his face,' she recalled. 'I realised it was moonlight, but it gave him a very pale, washed-out look.'

So, she picked him up and took him again to the spare room to sleep the rest of the night. 'As I carried him through the house, he felt so heavy, like a dead weight,' she said. 'I was cuddling him under the covers, but he felt cold and bony, stiff and unresponsive.'

Later, she stirred and reached over to put an arm round her son. But the bed was empty. 'I leapt up faster than I've ever leapt out of bed in my life,' she said. 'I was looking everywhere; under the bed, behind the door, in other rooms, but he wasn't there. His teddy was gone, so I thought he must've taken himself back to his room.'

Sure enough, there he was, asleep in his own bed. She gently woke him up to ask if he was okay and why he'd gone back to bed without telling her. *No, Mummy*, he murmured. *I didn't leave my bedroom.*

It turned out that the new nanny had checked on him just thirty minutes earlier, and he'd been fast asleep. The baby monitor in the nanny's room proved this also – its movement sensor hadn't been activated all night. 'I don't know what it was I took to bed that night,' said Natalie, 'but it wasn't Nate. It took me six months to get over that.'

Eventually, Natalie found a local psychic medium to come and 'spiritually cleanse' the house. She burned sage and left some crystals, and that worked for a while, until it didn't. Then a friend introduced her to a Methodist priest, who gave her a cross and holy water which she and the friend sprinkled while reciting the Lord's Prayer. Again, in the end, the discomfort returned.

It never occurred to Natalie to investigate her home's history. Like me, she was too concerned with the present to consider the past. But then a friend sent her a photograph of an old newspaper cutting with a faded picture of a big house that looked exactly like hers.

'Above the photograph was a short headline that read "Wirral

House of Horrors",' she said. 'I was like, oh my gosh, that's my house. At first, I didn't want to read it.'

—

Wirral Manor House was built in 1856 by a crooked account-ant with money he'd embezzled from his employers.[2] When he was convicted and transported to Australia, a local lord named Samuel Holland Moreton seized the property for himself. Moreton expanded the building, adding a courthouse where he and his steward, Robert Grace, presided over local matters. The court became known for its biased rulings and alleged coerced participation, generating considerable resentment across the community.

'This guy was notorious for holding the court as a form of entertainment for his rich friends,' said Natalie, who spent months researching local records of these men. 'They would get completely drunk and they would basically overcharge people, take their money, seize their property, and leave them destitute.'

There were even rumours, she claimed, that people had gone missing around the time they went to the court, never to be seen again. 'There were concerns at the time that people were killed to stop them testifying over where their assets had gone.'

In one local newspaper report from the early 1900s, Natalie read that Moreton was not only unkind to those he consid-ered of inferior status, but also to his family, especially his young daughters.

'On some days,' said Natalie, 'the sound of children singing still passes through parts of the house, especially in the stables and courtyard outside.'

We'd come back out into the stone courtyard, and it was lightly drizzling. She led me down some steep narrow steps into a lightless basement beneath the house that smelled of damp earth. 'I asked a spiritualist to come and see the house,' she said. 'When he came down here, he said he could sense the presence of children. He said children had spent a lot of time in the basement because they were scared to play with their toys in the main house.'

She crouched down and gestured towards a rectangular hole in the wall where a brick was missing. 'Later, when we were clearing out the space we found a loose brick here. Behind it was a perfectly preserved set of the game pick-up-sticks,' she said. 'The girls must've hidden them in the cavity to play with. It's just so sad.'

I looked into this but couldn't independently find any evidence for the vanished witnesses or the child cruelty. But there was more. 'In March 2020, we took the kids to the field to dig up worms for my husband's fishing hooks, and we pulled out this really thin, rusty old knife,' Natalie said.

She posted a photo of it on her Facebook page and, within days, the Wirral Archaeological Society got in touch. 'They told us under no circumstances should we dig anything else,' she said. 'They came over in full hazmat suits, worked on both ours and the adjacent land for several days, and found all sorts of things, from the insides of carts and chariots to bits of shields and arrowheads.'

The archaeologists came to an astonishing conclusion: that these fields were likely the lost site of the Battle of Brunanburh, one of the most significant battlefields of medieval Britain. Fought in 937 between the English king Æthelstan and an alliance of

Celtic and Viking invaders, it was a bloodbath. Æthelstan's army routed the intruders, in what was memorialised in the ancient poem 'Battle of Brunanburh' in the *Anglo-Saxon Chronicle*:

> Never yet as many people killed before this with sword's edge . . . since the east Angles and Saxons came up over the broad sea[1]

'They said it was an incredibly bloody battle, and historically very significant, but its exact location had always been a mystery,' Natalie said. One of the archaeologists, she added, told her that Vikings often adopted the names of fearsome animals. For her, this tallied with Nate's claims that a bear was living in his room.

Was the breath she heard that night in 2017 linked to the battle? She doesn't know, only that whatever it was that she sensed had a distinctly 'masculine energy'. 'I couldn't rule it out,' she said. 'Sometimes in this house, I don't know what to believe.'

'Do you still feel scared by the house, Natalie?' I asked. 'Have you ever thought of moving on?'

She looked at me with comic disgust. 'Good god, no. This is still my dream home. Most of the time, our experience here is beautiful. We've renovated, got rid of bits and pieces, changed everything. The place feels rejuvenated. It's just, now and again, you have this transient feeling of doom, and strange things happen.'

The gravel crunched beneath our feet as we walked round the house to the front, where my car was parked. It was getting late, and I had a long drive home. On the horizon, beyond the fields over which Æthelstan's armies once marched, the sun was turning the clouds to embers as the wind let out the last breaths of day.

Night was rousing, and with it whatever ancient energy slept beneath Wirral Manor House. If it really was ever there.

Natalie was looking up at her home, pensively. 'You know,' she said, 'as Nate grew up, a lot of the nastiest stuff died off, as if it had been somehow attached to *his* energy.'

I thought back to what Jason Bray had said: *The really strange thing about paranormal experiences is that children or teenagers seem particularly susceptible.*

I realised then that many of the scary stories Natalie had told me had involved her children in some way or other, especially her son. It seemed invasive to ask her about his mental health. Or, for that matter, hers.

Pamela Heath had said the mind, particularly in times of high stress, can do extraordinary things to meet our subconscious needs. Could something have happened to the boy that gave physical shape to his anxieties? A hard time at school, perhaps? Or picking up on, and internalising, a parent's anxieties over work, life or love?

The bear he saw in his room may have been the abiding energy of a Viking warrior slain on this ground centuries ago, sure. It could have been the memory of one of the many locals Samuel Moreton slighted here during his reign as Lord of the Hundred Court; or, indeed, one of the people who went missing around that time. It could be an accumulation of all those things, and more. Or maybe, it was just a teddy bear, an imaginary friend imbued with the fears and anxieties of a small boy adapting to a new home.

If Natalie's home was under the influence of, as Pamela called it, a 'layered place memory', what if the boy had been the one to channel it out of the past and into the present? Perhaps his mind had somehow entangled with his mother's to give form to both their fears, leaving her husband unperturbed.

As I drove slowly back down the gravel driveway, past the pond and the trees, I stopped at the gateway and looked back at the house in the rear-view mirror. I saw Natalie still standing there. Then she turned and vanished through her front door, as if slipping through a chink in the night, before it folded shut behind her.

Chapter 18

THE GEOPHYSICIST

By the time I returned from the Wirral, the smell was back. Although it was less of a surprise now. I had grown accustomed to its comings and goings, which had become so regular that it could have had its own key. I came to think of it as a reclusive, foul-breathed housemate whom I never saw and couldn't evict. One who drifted in and out of the house as he fancied, bumping about in empty rooms, leaving only his fetid odour behind when he came downstairs. Though the smell still seemed to move about from spot to spot and, just as Yeats observed, often appeared to vanish as suddenly as it arose. I was resigned to the assumption that, whatever it was, it would not be expelled lightly.

One Saturday night, Jody and I were recovering from an over-ambitious takeaway on the sofa, watching a Tom Cruise movie. Suddenly Jody sat up.

'What was that?' she snapped, shooting a troubled look towards the kitchen.

'What?'

'That noise.'

'What noise?'

'That rustling noise. And bumping. Are you telling me you can't hear that? In the kitchen.'

I muted the TV and listened.

'There's no noise,' I said dismissively, thinking how this felt strangely like the time she heard the doorbell. 'You're imagining it.'

Then I heard it. A faint but unmistakable scratching sound, like tiny nails on wood. Then there was a light thud. Then another. More scratching, then a crunch.

I glanced at Jody, who was staring at the kitchen doorway. Neither of us said a word. The crunching continued for a few seconds, then stopped abruptly. We held our breath, listening. The only sound was the low hum of the fridge.

'Maybe it's a mouse?' I suggested, trying to sound cool. But I didn't believe it. Mice don't make that kind of deliberate scratching sound.

Jody shook her head. 'No. It's bigger than a mouse.'

We waited, frozen in place, but the sound didn't return. After a few minutes, I slowly got up from the sofa and moved towards the kitchen. The kitchen was at the back of the living room, through an open doorway, over which I'd hung a curtain to defend against drafts. I reached for the curtain, took a deep breath, and swept it open.

The kitchen was empty. There was no sign of anything or anyone. I checked inside all the cupboards, in the drawers, even inside the fridge. Nothing. Jody stayed on the sofa.

'See?' I said with a victorious smile. 'It was nothing.'

But as I turned to leave, I heard another bump, and a frantic rustling. I knew then that it was coming from the bin, which was tucked away in a drawer under the sink.

I bent down and cautiously pulled open the drawer. The lid

of the bin was slightly askew. Not how I left it. I placed my hand around the handle and cautiously raised it up.

I saw it then, half hidden among the chicken nuggets and tea-bags and pesto pasta Jasmine hadn't finished that evening. A rat. A massive bloated rat with protruding yellow teeth that looked like tusks. Its long tail snaked through the rubbish and its skin strained against its matted grey fur.

I'd like to say that we both froze. I'd like to say our eyes met. And there, amongst the rubbish of both our lives, we shared a fleeting moment of profound mutual understanding and respect. I'd like to say that in her eyes I saw a frightened, vulnerable animal doing the best she could do with the life she'd been given. And that, in mine, she saw the same.

But in real life, rats in bins are not metaphors for the struggle of existence in an unforgiving world, but simply . . . revolting, pestilent rats in bins.

Anyway, there wasn't time to think anything beyond 'Fffeuck!' I made a sound I'd never made before – somewhere between a yelp and a retch. The rat hissed. Then she whipped her tail for lever-age, squirmed free of an old avocado shell and jumped at my face. As she did so, she let out a high-pitched squeak. I recoiled and, in impulsive defence, swung the bin lid like a tennis racquet. I only caught her tail. She landed on the bin's edge. She squeaked again, whirled round and flung herself over the bin to the back of the drawer and vanished behind the kitchen cabinet.

'What the hell happened?' called Jody from the sofa.

'You don't want to know,' I replied, breathing heavily.

'It was a rat, wasn't it?' she said.

We shared a look.

'Fuck this, I'm going to bed,' she said. 'Make sure the door is properly closed before you come up. If that thing gets up into the bedroom I'm never coming back here again.' She picked up her mug and left the room. I listened to her footsteps disappear up the stairs. Then I stood in the living room in silence.

I know rats are a part of life. I know you're never more than six feet from a rat in London, where it's said they outnumber humans by around two to one. They live in the sewers and the shadows and only come out to eat our food and chew through our homes. They can bite six times a second, and their teeth are stronger than iron. They carry diseases such as Hantavirus, leptospirosis and lungworm. I know the life expectancy of a rat is approximately one year. In that time, it may have sex twenty times a day and has the potential of producing 15,000 offspring with one mate. I also know that rats can map out entire rooms in their minds, a group is called a mischief, and they laugh when tickled. Male rats sing after sex.

Rats. I hate them. The thought of them in my home – under my floorboards, in my walls – made my skin writhe. If they were behind the scratching, could they also be the source of the smells? But the smell I'd been living alongside was not the smell of something alive.

—

'Blimey,' the ratcatcher grunted, wiping sweat from his brow. It was the afternoon after The Night of the Rat, and we were kneeling in the garden, peering down a manhole we'd just discovered under the decking by the back door. 'It's a proper rabbit warren down there.'

I squinted over the edge of the brick-built hole and was relieved to see he didn't mean this literally. Through the gloom, I could make out a spaghetti junction of pipes snaking into the darkness, disappearing under the house and away. 'Sewer line runs right under your garden,' he pointed a latex-gloved finger down the hole. 'Bunch of smaller pipes branching off, going to the main line in the street. But there's one . . .' he trailed off. 'One that's bone dry. That's your culprit, I reckon.'

'What does that mean?' I was confused. 'Where does it go?'

'Nowhere, anywhere, who knows?' he shrugged. 'It probably went somewhere once, but not any more.'

He shone the torch on his phone into the murk. 'Can you see the earth in it? Water would've flushed that out if it was in use. That earth has probably been scuffed back by rodents digging inside.'

I felt a glob of nausea rise inside me. 'Digging where?'

He went on to explain with enthusiasm that the Victorians, in their rush to throw up more homes to feed London's housing boom, tended to lay little or no foundations under terraced streets. The logic, he said, was that a long row of conjoined houses would hold itself up, spreading its collective weight so it wouldn't sink into the soil.

'The problem is,' he said, 'rats are very good burrowers. They can dig in any direction. My guess is they've come in along the sewer, found this old pipe, maybe chewed a hole in it somewhere under your house, and burrowed upwards until they came out under your floor.'

The glob found my oesophagus. 'So, what, are we going to have to pull up all the floorboards to find the hole?' I asked.

He shook his head. 'No, that won't be necessary. I have a rat flap in the van.'

A rat flap is a metal cylinder with a one-way valve that fits inside disused pipes. It is designed to allow water – or rats – out, but nothing in. 'The flap means rats can get out of the pipe to go home or find food, but can't come back,' he said. 'You don't want them getting stuck up there.'

One hundred pounds later, the ratcatcher had inserted the rat flap and left enough poison in various nooks to make an elephant need a lie-down. 'Hopefully the rat is already gone,' he said as he left. 'Or, if not, it soon will be.' Then he added, 'You have to wait and see.'

—

I've always considered myself a rational person. But my powers of rationality were dissolving fast amid this assault of new experiences. The smells, the electrics, the water, the strange noises – it was as if the house itself was unsettled. Even the pest encounters felt a little abnormal, if only by proximity to one another – like a series of Bible-style micro plagues sent, or beckoned, by some snarling, malevolent force hiding inside my home.

As absurd as that sounded, I'd made a promise to myself to keep an open mind when it came to what happened here. So, a week later, when the friend of a friend mentioned something called 'geopathology' in the kitchen of a birthday party, I scrawled it on my hand in biro.

'Geo-what?' I half shouted over the music.

'Geopathology,' said the friend's friend, whose name I'd already forgotten. 'It's the idea that the land beneath a house could, like, disrupt the Earth's natural vibrations. And that can affect the people living there.'

'You don't strike me as the New-Agey type,' I said.

'No, no, this is scientific,' he shook his head, leaning in so I could smell his breath. 'Well, there is science behind it. It's about the Earth's electromagnetic fields. And if they're disrupted in a certain place, it can make people sick. You said there was a sewer running beneath your house?'

'I think that's how the rat got in.'

'Well, some people believe water running beneath a house can influence our health, and even affect animal behaviour.'

He swigged from a can of lager. 'They call it geopathic stress.'

The basic theory is this: the Earth has a natural vibration, but things like underground rivers, drainage pipes, sewers, mineral deposits and even geological faults distort this vibration. Spending any significant time above such a place can affect your health and behaviour. Hardcore proponents even reckon it can be linked to things like miscarriage and cancer. However, these claims are largely dismissed by the mainstream scientific community due to a lack of credible research and evidence.

—

A quick internet search will reveal no shortage of people who, like pay-as-you-go exorcists, will charge you to cleanse your home of geopathic stress. Their websites make statements ranging from the vague ('Land can soak up the energy of something negative and foster bad situations') to the vapid ('Because there is so much energy stored in land, it can be contradictory to your goals and intentions') to the cynically irresponsible (I found one website that claimed, without evidence, that geopathic stress is present in 'the majority of people who are suicidal', and 'about 80% of people who get divorced'). They'll offer treatments like sprinkling moon-energised water or laying crystals to create healing 'grids' around the property. More serious ones will use divining rods to 'dowse' your land to locate sources of negative energy. The word pseudo-science comes up a lot.

But for the career scientists exploring the biophysical inter-play between the environment and human health, claims like these are damaging. At best, they manipulate legitimate scientific findings for profit; at worst, they prey on vulnerable individuals, offering false hope and potentially delaying or preventing access to effective treatments.

Professor Gerhard Hacker is an Austrian medical biologist and molecular morphologist who has devoted much of his career to exploring ways in which our bodies interact with the world. He is a prolific author and researcher with a PhD in natural sciences from the University of Salzburg, and a diploma in endocrinology from the University of London. He's held research positions at prestigious institutions like London's Hammersmith Hospital and the University of Uppsala's Institute of Pathology in Sweden, and has lectured extensively on topics ranging from hospital ethics to molecular diagnostics.

In one 2008 study entitled 'Geopathic Stress Zones and Their Influence on the Human Organism', he and colleagues explored how even the subtlest variations in the Earth's magnetic field could affect human health.[1]

To do this, they placed one group of people in a location identified through dowsing as a 'geopathic stress zone', and a control group in a 'neutral zone'. Then, using something called gas discharge visualisation technology, they captured images of the electrical discharge emanating from each participant's fingertips – a real phenomenon, based on the Kirlian effect, thought to be influenced by various biological processes such as cellular activity. The idea was that a change in the electrical 'glow' suggested a change in physical or emotional state.

The result: the energy field affecting the participants in the geopathic stress zone reduced significantly, while that of the control group did not. 'Our study has shown that certain areas above the ground can indeed induce stress,' the paper concluded. 'Such zones might cause distress ("malignant stress") even when present for a short time.'

The paper, published in the German medical journal *Forschende Komplementärmedizin*, went on to suggest that 'location-dependent stress' may, 'if present for a prolonged time . . . suppress the immune system'. Other possible consequences of living in a geopathic stress zone, it hypothesised, include poorer sleep quality, slower healing capacity and even increased aggression towards partners.

This was all very well. But it didn't help to explain whether the sewer beneath my house was impacting my mental health. So, I sent Professor Hacker an email.

A week later, he replied, apologising for the delay; he'd been snorkelling in Egypt. 'First, it is necessary that you should know that I am retired already and haven't worked in the field for several years,' he said, directing me to several papers he had written on the subject. But after some gentle coercion, he agreed to talk in a few days. We arranged to speak via video call.

'Have you been sleeping badly?' he cut in as soon as I told him my story.

I said I had. He thought for a moment.

'Geopathic stress does not, in my opinion, happen as often as dowsers want you to think,' he told me straight away. 'There is a huge industry selling devices and other remedies that claim to combat geopathic stress. These things work similarly to some pseudo medicines in homeopathy. If you believe in it, there might be some positive effect. It's no different to putting a drop of energy water on a sugar cube – pure placebo.'

He made air quotes with his fingers when he said, 'energy water'. Then his tone shifted. 'But I believe geopathic stress is a real phenomenon. And while houses under a strong influence of geopathic stress are few and far between, some do have it. I really would not want to live in one.'

Then he directed me to another study, in which colleagues at the University of Zurich's veterinary medicine faculty measured melatonin sulphate levels in the urine of two groups of cows, one in a supposed geopathic stress zone and another not.[2] 'Those cows standing on areas of geopathic stress had less melatonin in their urine,' he said. 'This not only showed clear negative effects on milk quality but indirectly indicates that there might be a negative influence on the immune system and quality of sleep.'

I wanted to know what the biophysical mechanisms that might cause geopathic stress are exactly. Could any of them apply to my home? 'Well, first of all, there are many factors that we think can cause geopathic stress,' he said, 'and all of them are hypotheses – we do not know for sure – but I have collaborated with many physicists, geophysicists and hydrophysicists over the years to find out how geopathology might affect humans, and it is a complex thing.'

Gerhard had much smoother skin than his years should afford. Somewhere in his late sixties, he put this down to exercise and a diet untainted by the ravages of meat – he is an ethical vegan. Despite his science background, he said he had a spiritual side but that it does not impinge, as far as is possible, on his scientific work. For example, he thinks the ideas around Hartman and Curry grids – that the Earth is cut up by a network of invisible energy lines that influence human health – are swivel-eyed quackery. 'These cannot exist,' he said. 'It is not possible from what is present in the ground.' He believes the powers of dowsing, which involves waving around a forked stick or 'divining rod' to detect subterranean water sources, are overblown.

But geopathology, in his view, may have legitimate biomechanical underpinnings. One is that subterranean waterways can contain certain metallic ions and particles that influence electromagnetic fields as they swirl about.

'But how do they affect *us*?' I asked.

'Well, one possible explanation is the presence of magnetite crystals in the brain,' he said.

'As in . . . magnets?' I said. 'In our brains?'

'Yes. Magnetite is the most magnetic mineral on Earth and recent studies have shown crystals of it exist in the human brain.'

In fact, in 1992, it was discovered that our brains are stuffed with magnets.

It was a startling revelation made by a team of American scientists, led by the famed Caltech geophysicist Joseph Kirschvink.[3]

They looked inside the brains of seven dead Californians and detected billions of tiny crystal grains of the stuff, some barely wider than a strand of DNA, in areas of the brain that control decision-making, sensory perception, movement, memory, balance, emotion, personality and more. They were everywhere.

Closer analysis found these crystals to be strikingly similar to those found in magnetotactic bacteria, which use magnetite crystals to navigate lakes and seas by sensing the Earth's magnetic field, like a biological compass. It has also been discovered in brains across the animal kingdom, and is believed to explain why birds, turtles and bats can orient the Earth.

But it was not until 2019 that a team of scientists, led again by Kirschvink, found 'clear cut, quantifiable and reproducible' evidence that we do, in fact, subconsciously respond to changes in Earth's magnetic fields.[4] How or why magnetite gets into our brains remains a mystery. Some scientists say it's in the pollution we breathe, others that it could be the vestige of a long-defunct internal navigation system.

What does Gerhard think? 'It could be a kind of relic from the evolutionary past,' he said. 'But if that is the case, those particles should not exist in such a high quantity any more.'

It is more likely, he thought, that they do still have some kind of function. 'Maybe they provide a framework for explaining how certain qualities of geopathic zones affect the body,' he said. 'Magnetite is over one million times more magnetic than any other biological material. So, I think it makes sense. But there is no concrete evidence linking the presence of magnetite in the brain to negative health effects. There is still a lot more work to be done before we fully understand it.'

'So, could the sewer beneath my house have influenced my emotional health?' I asked.

'It is possible,' he said. 'But, like I said, it depends on a lot of factors. You have been in a stressful, depressing situation, and such situations can be easily influenced by many things. And geopathy can be a part of it. It may cause insomnia. It might even influence your mind in a way that may cause depression. The immune system is likely to be inhibited. People might get very ill.'

He looked at me intensely. And although he was 700 miles away in Austria, for a split second, it felt like he was with me in the room. 'But it is also important to remember that when you are in a stressful time, small stresses can feel bigger,' he said gently. 'That itself may cause insomnia and other issues, which may induce further depression and further problems. So, you must be careful to consider everything that is happening. Do not focus all your energies on just one thing.'

⁓

After our conversation, I struggled to dredge the image of that sewer from my mind. It was as if, now I knew of the magnets in my brain, they were pulling septic thoughts towards them. Cooking in the kitchen, I winced when I imagined the sewage flowing beneath my feet, sloshing and gurgling with other people's waste. I pictured swarms of rats writhing through it, sniffing, scratching, hunting. In my mind's eye, a highway of dirt and disease was coursing below my house. More than once, the 'sewer of slime' scene in *Ghostbusters II* came to mind – one of innumerable cultural influences that magnified my anxieties.

I suppose, in hindsight, I didn't much consider the bigger

picture – that there are few places you can go in London where there is not a sewer line somewhere below.

But it was true that I had been sleeping badly. It was also clear that my mental health had grown worse since moving into the house. But could this all really be linked to a disruption in electromagnetic activity flowing up from beneath the ground?

And what about the house's past? Was it purely a coincidence that a man capable of such evil had lived above this potential source of geopathic stress? No. It felt perverse to even imagine a connection between the sewer and the murderer who resided here before me; that perhaps he was affected by forces emanating from beneath the earth. And then what? That he was in some way 'turned' by the house? If so, was the house infecting me? No. It was a ludicrous insinuation. No, no, a thousand times no. *I am not living inside a Stephen King novel*, I told myself again and again. *Aman Vyas and I have nothing in common but this space. Different times, different lives. We are different men!*

Chapter 19

PRISON MEANS PRISON

In the mugshot, he smirks like the law is a puzzle he has already solved. It is the expression of a confident man. The camera holds no power over him; he says that with a faint curl of his lips. His eyes, though sunken and tired from a long flight, betray a glint of amusement, as if this whole process were beneath him. His hair is no longer the 'bobbly' crop it once was but has thinned into a patchy widow's peak. The youthful blackness of his beard is infiltrated by a cluster of white wisps about his chin. In the mugshot, he is not the young man he was in Walthamstow. He is thirty-four. I wonder how often he smirks like this now.

This image was taken on 5 October 2019 at Heathrow police station, just after Shaleena Sheikh read him his rights, and before he called his mother. There are no other images of Aman Vyas in the public domain. None, at least, in which you can clearly see his face.

All mugshots tell a story. From the bewildered glance of the first-time offender to the oily stare of a seasoned criminal, they offer a glimpse into a moment of crisis. At the mercy of the police, the subjects usually have had little time to prepare a pose. For the newsworthy offenders, they may not yet realise that this picture will be their lasting message to the world. It is made for, and will forever belong to, the public. Vyas, on the other hand, had weeks to prepare for his. And this is what he came up with.

I have looked at this picture many times since learning of the man who lived here. Too many times. I have lost days of my life thinking about him, talking about him, reading newspaper reports and court transcripts describing him. But how much did I really know? Who was he and how, apart from stalking women late at night, did he spend his time? In many ways, the absence of information about him was more telling than the few obtainable facts. I realised that, all this time, I had been fixated, not on a person, but on an idea. A story. I knew *what* he was. He was a rapist and murderer. But I knew nothing about *who* he was. Was Michelle's sister Ann right when she so poignantly told him in court, 'You weren't born that way, something's turned you into what you are.'

It was impossible to say with any certainty what he, or his life, was like, let alone what went on inside the house when he was here. In months of enquiry into Vyas's past, I found no one who could be described as his friend. I could find barely anyone who remembered him at all, save for a local shopkeeper who recalled serving him once or twice. He was still a ghost.

That is not surprising, given the relatively short time he lived in London, in an area that has – in the many years since – regenerated significantly. I can't even be sure exactly when, or for how long, he was living in my house.

Here's what I do know: he drifted into Walthamstow in September 2007 and then vanished in June 2009. In that time, I know from detective Steve Lynch that he was associated with several addresses in the same area of Walthamstow. Not surprisingly, Steve didn't remember the particulars of all his homes. They just weren't crucial to the investigation, as Vyas was years gone by the time he was identified. In one of them, Steve said he lived with his brother Raja, who himself had left England by the time Vyas was apprehended. Another was the home of his mysterious girlfriend, where he often stayed. Either, for all I knew, could be my house. The closest I have to anything concrete are the recollections of neighbours like Jackie, a teacher, and Michael, a French polisher. They remember him being here around the time of the fires, on Tuesday 12 February and Tuesday 10 June 2008.

'I remember it clear as day,' Michael had told me. 'Your house was on fire. Flames and black smoke were pouring out of the top windows. The fire engines were there, blue lights flashing. It was chaos. All the neighbours had come out of their houses to watch. And there he was, leaning against a wall across the street just watching.'

'Did you speak to him?' I asked.

'He nodded to me, but we didn't speak,' said Michael. 'I was more worried the fire was going to spread across into my house, to be honest. But I can remember he seemed very calm considering the place he lived in was burning down.'

'Are you absolutely sure it was him?' I pressed. 'You don't think there's a chance you could be mistaken?'

'It was him,' Michael said emphatically. 'I can remember my own neighbour. I walked past him in the street enough times. He'd say hello, or nod politely. But he never gave much more than that.'

Michael said he remembered the first time he linked his mysterious neighbour to the E17 Night Stalker, then called the Calendar Killer. 'We were watching a news segment on TV about the attacks that'd happened down the road, and they showed the photofit of the suspect,' he said. 'Jackie turned to me and said, "Michael, that's him from the Fire House." I agreed that it looked just like him. It was such a likeness.'

When the CCTV images flashed up, there was something else they recognised too: the jacket with two white stripes down the arm.

'Didn't you report him?' I wondered.

'Well, it was just the police photofit and a grainy CCTV image at first,' he said. 'We weren't a hundred per cent sure it was him at the time, and I hadn't seen him in months by then. Then, a year or two later I can remember seeing police cars coming to the house, and coppers coming and going. That's when it clicked.'

It would be another ten years before Michael would get a proper look at his face – via the mugshot released after Vyas's arrest. 'We'd forgotten all about it, life had moved on,' Michael said. 'But I remember seeing that picture in the news and it all came back. He looked older than I remembered him, less hair, but it was him. Other neighbours, who have since moved on, they remembered him too.'

Michael paused, then he said it again, this time as if each word were its own sentence. 'It. Was. Him.'

—

I wanted to know more about who Vyas was living with – or staying with – in my house. Perhaps they could shed light on what he was like, and what caused the fires. The trouble was, of the few neighbours left who had lived on the street in 2008, none seemed to know who they were. Some said it was a single mother of Asian descent with children of a variety of ages. Nobody could say how many children, nor how old they were at the time, just that they argued a lot. Others remembered a small group of South Asian men, as well as a series of Eastern Europeans. No dates were forthcoming. It was all just too long ago, everybody said. People come, and people go.

I paid a visit to the local records office, tucked away in a dusty attic at the ancient Vestry House Museum, to check the electoral role. There, in a little red-bound book, I ran my finger down the list of voters registered at my address. To my surprise, I read at least one name for every single year between 1889 and 2008 before, abruptly, the trail stopped dead. Between 2008 and 2016, nobody was registered to vote at the property until the family I bought the house from moved in. It was as if, for those eight years, the house was adrift, without a single person tethered to it. It was almost like, from the moment those fires tore through it, it ceased to exist.

But it *did* exist. Despite attempts to erase it – first with fire in February 2008, then again in June – it stood. Somebody had tried to burn it down. Twice. What exactly had happened? Who had been in the house when the fires started? How did they start? So I went back to the Fire Brigade for the incident reports filed by the firefighters on the scene. Two days later, they landed in my inbox. Much of the information mirrored what I already knew from the Freedom of Information request: dates, call-out times, categories of fire.

Then, at the very bottom of the page was a section entitled 'supposed motive of the fire'. And there, like a matchhead struck in the dark, one word sent my pulse racing: 'deliberate'.

So the fire had not been an accident. Not an electrical fault, not a cigarette in bed, not an overheated plug-in blanket. *Deliberate.*

'Heat source and combustibles brought together deliberately,' the duty commander had written. It didn't elaborate on what those combustibles were exactly, only that the first thing to catch light was 'bedding'.

Somebody, it seemed, had intentionally set fire to the bed and left. But why? Who of sound mind would torch their own house? Assuming, that is, they were of sound mind.

—

There was, of course, one other option to help me get to the truth. An option that had crouched, muttering, in the recesses of my mind since I learned of my home's past. Every time it crawled towards the light, I forced it back.

'You should totally meet him,' friends had told me. 'Don't you want to know what he'll say? I want to know what he's like. You *have* to meet him.'

I did not want to meet him – not least for the throat-tightening reason that he knew where I lived. But more than that, I did not want to look him in the eyes and risk seeing a monster – or worse, a man. I did not want to offer him the power of knowing he still held sway over someone's thoughts, even from behind bars. But most of all, I did not want to give him a voice. He'd had a banquet of opportunities to deny, prevaricate and dance his way around the facts, and he'd feasted on it. I didn't want to offer him another.

But if I truly wanted to understand what had happened in my home in 2008, Vyas was my last and only option. So, with a knot in my gut, I applied to the Ministry of Justice for a meeting with the prisoner.

Reaching a prisoner in Britain is not as easy as you might think. Here, prison means *prison*. That means contact with the outside world is strictly limited. Internet access is always supervised, and only allowed for rehabilitation purposes. Social media use is blanket-banned.[1] Meeting with friends and family is encouraged but tightly controlled – an inmate must submit a contact list to the prison's security office, where each name is vetted before they are allowed to visit. A guard is always in the room.

For journalists, the rules are ironclad. You must approach them via the government's 'Find a Prisoner' service. Your email is printed out and delivered to their cell on a piece of paper. Once they have granted permission for their information to be shared, you can begin the process of communication. Any communication is governed by PSI 37/2010, a 'prison service instruction' that sets out the rules for prisoners who want to speak to journalists, or vice versa.

Dear Mr Vyas,

My Name is Matthew Blake, a journalist researching a story about the homes and routines of people convicted of serious crimes.

I understand that there are restrictions on what we can discuss regarding your case. However, I am curious about your life in Walthamstow, and anything from that time you would care to share. Can you tell me about your social life and connections in Walthamstow? What did you like to do with your time when living in the area? Were you happy in Walthamstow?

I would especially like to ask you about the houses you lived in. What were they like? What details can you remember about the rooms, the atmosphere, or any routines you may have had? I understand there was a fire at one house you lived in during your time in Walthamstow – do you have any recollection of that event?

I am also interested in learning more about you. Would you like to tell me anything about your life prior to coming to Britain?

If you are willing to share any information or reflections with me, I would appreciate your cooperation. I will report any response you send me fairly and accurately.

Sincerely,

Sent. Now, all I could do was wait.

—

Meanwhile, the house revealed more scars of abuse and neglect. One evening I noticed a jagged chip on the dining-room wall, too high to have been accidental – a piece of furniture hurled in fury, perhaps? Then there was the damp patch creeping up beneath the bay window because somebody forgot to insert an air brick to let the underfloor breathe. The original stairs had been knocked out, spun round and rebuilt with medievally low headroom. One former owner, in a botched renovation, had even encased the cast-iron downpipe, connecting the upstairs toilet to the sewer, in concrete.

'Disaster waiting to happen, that,' the plumber told me. 'If it's not done properly, concrete can trap moisture against the iron, and the alkalinity can eat away at the pipe. If there's any salt in that mix, it'll rust out even faster. If it was a plumber, he should be bloody excommunicated! Banned from the trade for life.'

Whoever's incompetence it was, I paid through the nose for it: a chemical reaction that caused an insidious crack, and eventually, a hole that wept rusty brown sewage through the wall I shared with my neighbour.

It was as if the house itself was bleeding.

The biggest bruise of all, though, was the fire patch on the bedroom floor. It wasn't just unsightly. It gave the room a faint but constant aroma of old barbecues.

It felt like an awful lot to take on by myself. Some mornings, when I awoke from another fitful sleep, the emptiness of my house could fill me with a loneliness so intense that it was frightening.

My darkest fears always visited me at night. More than once I was awoken, not by a sound but by the most focused silence I've ever experienced. But it wasn't nothing. Something was there – less an *absence* of sound than the *presence* of silence. It was a living, yearning, screaming thing that drowned out all external noise and poisoned rational thought. It replaced thinking.

In those moments, the tick-tock of my heart turned into a countdown without numbers. I would lie in the darkness listening for irregularities, skips, double beats, and a cold dread curled through me: *am I dying?* Not in the vague sense that all adults are biologically dying. Death was coming for me, and it was coming at night. Perhaps not tonight, or tomorrow. But it *felt* close. None of this went through my mind when I stayed at Jody's, or anywhere else. It was a sickness of the house; I sensed it. The house was making me sick.

Alone in bed, I was haunted by thoughts of dying at night while Jasmine was there. I imagined her finding me, shaking me, talking to my stiffening body. I wondered how long she'd survive in this house until someone came. If they came.

So, to make it easier for them to gain entry when it happened,

I would leave the latch off the front door before heading up to bed. I made sure I never left a knife out overnight, or shoes on the stairs; nothing that could hurt a child alone in a home. I asked Jody to message me each morning, just in case. 'If I don't reply by lunchtime, send help,' I told her. 'Nick has a spare key.'

She didn't laugh at me or call me mad. She just did as I asked and reassured me. 'I've read that it's quite common for separated parents to develop death anxiety,' she said. 'It's called thanatophobia. It'll get easier, I know it will.'

—

But it wasn't getting easier. Barely a few nights after she said that to me the house turned on me once more as I slept. It happened on a night like every other night the house had tried to frighten me: quiet and still and dark.

I was home alone, sleeping off another day, when I was jolted awake by a new sound. Not an errant doorbell, or a shower. This time it was a metallic thud, followed by a soft, circular whirr, like something rolling.

For a moment I lay completely still. Not breathing. Not blinking. Just listening. The whirr slowed.

I turned my head.

There on the chest of drawers, a ten-pence coin was spinning through its last dying moments of motion. It shivered in the moonlight, wavered and then, in an agonizingly slow wobble, it dropped flat with a dull *clink*. Tails up.

Had I left it there? Maybe. I had emptied my pockets before bed, hadn't I? I couldn't remember. A ten-pence piece. Just lying there as if it had always been there. *Had it?*

I pushed myself up onto my elbows. The duvet felt too heavy; the room too cold. The coin glinted.

I checked the clock: 5:23 a.m. Almost exactly the same time as when the radio turned itself on.

Then I heard something. The sound of footsteps. I counted four of them, quick like a patter, each with a creak, then fading as if running away. They had come from above, through the ceiling. Was someone in the attic?

Nobody can be up there, I thought. *There's not even enough head-room for a grown person to stand up.*

I'd only been into the attic a handful of times since moving in. The only way up was through a trapdoor above the landing, via a folding ladder that you pulled down with a string.

I climbed out of bed, took the emergencies hammer from the bedside drawer, and tiptoed, barefoot, to the door. As I stepped out onto the landing, something like a draft – a cold movement of air – stroked my cheek. Seconds later I was standing under the trap-door. It was closed, just as it had been when I went to bed. I knew I had to check. I had to see for myself what had made that noise.

I heard the same patter of footsteps again. *One. Two. Three. Four.* It sounded like a child running.

The ladder gave way to a yank of the string, letting out a reluctant creak as I pulled it down to meet the landing floor. The cold rungs hurt my bare feet as I climbed. I reached out a trembling hand to the trap door, pushed, and lifted my head through the rectangle of light into sheer darkness.

The air was different up there – denser, laced with something old. I blinked into the pitch, waiting for my eyes to adjust, but the dark held on.

I hauled myself through the opening, breath clouding in front of me, and crouched on the boards. All I could hear was my own heart, ticking.

Then I felt it – a pressure, somewhere above me. Not a sound. Not a shift in the air. Just a sense. A presence.

As my eyes began to make sense of the shapes – boxes, beams, sagging insulation – I saw a shape. But it wasn't a shape, more a patch of something that didn't belong in there. Too dark to be shadow – too black, too infinitely deep. It didn't move. It didn't flicker or seethe. It just hung there like a hole in the world, sucking my thoughts towards it.

I forgot about the coin and the clock. I wanted to shout – but who would come? I wanted to run – but where?

So I just stared up at it, unable to move, or think. Just like in the fire dream. That same paralysis. That same invisible weight pinning me to the spot.

This isn't real, I told myself. *This isn't happening. It's a dream.* I squeezed my eyes shut and shook my head. *It's a dream. It's a dream.*

But was it a dream? I'm no more certain now of what I saw than I was that night. Because when I opened my eyes – it was still there. Only now, it seemed denser than before, and closer.

I was staring into it, as if peering down a tunnel. But there was no light at its end; it had no end. And then, from somewhere inside that darkness . . . something stared back.

I couldn't see it. Only feel it. Eyes watching. Was it a ghost? *No. I don't believe in ghosts.* I don't know what it was, just that something was in the house with me. Something so very sad, and angry. My thoughts writhed and gnawed like a rat inside my skull. I thought of the grow house, and the people, or person, who lived here, in the heat of the hydroponic lights, to tend the crop. I thought about the fires, and about Vyas, and wondered if *he* ever came up here at night. As I thought of these things the darkness deepened before me. And the eyes I couldn't see stared harder.

There, in that silence, I felt absolute terror. Not just in the room, but inside me.

I couldn't look away. I could only accept it. Let it in.

Suddenly, something within me jolted and I blinked and a hand that didn't seem to belong to me thrust out to the cord dangling from the attic's central beam. I tugged it and the bulb clicked and filled the attic with a light that hurt my eyes. Dazed, I looked about. Nothing was there. The dark patch was gone. Just a few dusty boxes with words like *photo albums* and *old house stuff* scrawled in Sharpie across their sides, a half-empty carton of bathroom tiles and an old shoe that wasn't mine.

I returned down the ladder with tears in my eyes and cowered in my bed.

I'd imagined stepping from the shadow of divorce into a house wreathed in light and happiness. It would be a place where I would entertain gaggles of friends and cook lavish pasta dinners with fresh herbs grown in pots by the window. A place where I could give Jasmine the magical childhood all children deserve, where she could play teachers with her doll babies and host playdates with her classmates. We'd throw raucous birthday parties for her in the summer and carve pumpkins at Halloween. Father Christmas would squeeze down our chimney each December and the tooth fairy would build a tiny cottage of teeth at the bottom of our garden. I wanted the sort of house that wrapped itself around you like a hug, not a chokehold.

Chapter 20

THE GIRL IN THE WINDOW

A few nights later, I woke up at 3 a.m. to the sound of scurrying somewhere above my head. It was soft at first but building steadily. It wasn't a gnawing or a squeaking, but a rhythmic scratching that seemed to be coming from inside the house. I blinked sleep from my eyes and listened through the darkness. Rats! It had to be rats. I could hear them scuttling inside the walls, under the floorboards, in the ceiling and the roof. The noise was growing into a cacophony of little claws on wood and plaster. They were everywhere, I was sure of it. But how did they get upstairs? Where did they come from? What was their plan? If they were in the walls, then soon they would be dropping from the vents, swarming the stairs, the floors, my bed.

I'd read that rats become sexually mature after about ten weeks and can have litters of up to twelve pups a month. Exponentially speaking, that's about a battalion a year. Perhaps the one I'd met was only the messenger, the scout, the bravest hero of a rat kingdom already here, feeding off my crumbs.

There! I saw a shadow move in the corner of the room. I grabbed the nearest object – a gifted hardback of *Jaws* by Peter Benchley on the bedside table – and hurled it at the wall. 'GET OUT!' I shouted. 'GET OUT OF MY HOUSE!'

Then, as abruptly as it had woken me, the noise changed. The scurrying morphed into a steady drumming. As my senses recalibrated, a hot shame washed over me . . . It wasn't rats. It was the weather. Just a thunderstorm lashing the windows and roof with rain and hail. But there, lying in the dark, I knew. This house was twisting my perceptions, turning every creak and groan into a manifestation of my own anxieties. I knew then that I was losing my grip, slipping towards a paranoia as insidious as black mould.

—

In the morning, sunshine spilled into the bedroom and I wondered if it had all been another bad dream. I scrutinised the room, trying to capture last night before it was lost forever in the basement of my brain. Then I spotted *Jaws* on the floor. And there, about a metre up, was a scratch where the book must have connected with the wall. There was something else too. The book had chipped away a thumbnail of paint and some plaster behind that, revealing an image. It looked like an eye. I got out of bed and peered closer at the chip. It was definitely an eye.

I scratched the paint with my fingernail. More plaster crumbled to the floor. Gradually, the image grew from one eye, to two, then a face and a body: a little black nose, two big black ears, red shorts, yellow shoes. It was the only rodent I'll accept inside my house – Mickey Mouse. Once, before the murderer and the fires, this must have been a child's bedroom.

Now that I'd started, I couldn't stop. I didn't want to think about last night. So instead, I found a decorator's scraper downstairs and began peeling. Soon I had a full geometric motif of Mickeys, all laughing jollily back at me. Not mockingly, though; invitingly.

—

I started immediately, stripping layer from layer of wallpaper as far as the wall would consent. I washed and scraped and ripped with my hands, and the paper rolled off onto the floor. I became breathless and frantic. The smell of old paste and something faintly floral filled the room as I peeled away the Mickeys to find another pattern beneath. Then another, and another. Something was happening. In all, I found four different wallpapers, each perfectly preserved behind its replacement: Mickey Mouses (the 2000s?) gave way to forest green with gold fleurs-de-lis (the 1990s?). Then there was orange under silver Deco-style diamonds (the 1970s?), and under that a layer of white with flowers and strawberries (surely not the Second World War!).

None of them covered the entire room. The 2008 fire had eaten all the way through them in places. In others, I found telltale singe marks that the flames had only licked. In the places that the fire hadn't reached, the patterns had lain quietly beneath the plaster, like fossilised footprints under layers of ancient mud.

It felt so intimate to strip this old room down to its barest state. With each layer that rolled off, I was momentarily transported back into somebody else's bedroom; where they slept, dreamed, undressed, made love.

As darkness fell, I stood back to take it all in, the room's peeled skins lying in curls about my feet. It was as if the house was letting me in on a secret no one else alive knew.

It was curiously intoxicating. I wanted more. Then something tugged at my attention. The white-plastic windowsill was faintly askew. How had I not noticed this before? I could not let it go uninvestigated. So, I gave it a tug. It loosened a little. I wedged my fingers under the lip of the sill and gave it a heave. With a snap of glue, it popped off.

Beneath it lay a second windowsill of dark, aged wood. The light was retreating, but I could still just about make out a mark in the corner of the sill. Something was etched into the wood. It was a heart about the size of a pound coin, pierced by an arrow. Inside the arrow were two letters – an 'S' and a 'K', bound together by a '+'. And above that, there was a name:

Suhanee

I think it was Suhanee; the name was barely legible, almost completely worn away by cleaning rags and wistful elbows. But it was definitely a name, apparently Hindu in origin. I ran my fingers over the inscription, tracing its faint outline. I could feel goosebumps creeping up my spine. Who was Suhanee? How long had her name been here? And who was 'K'? Was it love? A forgotten childhood crush?

For days, I couldn't prize this mystery dreamer from my imagination. I pictured her, an eighties girl, curled up on her Memphis-patterned duvet and listening to Jason Donovan on cassette – elbows on the sill, chin in hands, gazing out into the night sky for shooting stars. For a nanosecond I could smell nail varnish and hairspray.

I wondered what happened to her. She could be a grandmother by now, for all I knew. Does she remember this house fondly?

Did her parents punish her for vandalising the windowsill? Maybe that's why they glued the plastic trimming on top of it – to erase her forbidden love from sight, and mind. I wondered if it worked out with K.

Then it occurred to me: what if I could just ask her myself? It was clearly a long shot, but maybe I could find her. Now that I thought about it, what of all the others? This house was more than a hundred years old. Dozens of people must have lived here through the decades. Who was here when Queen Victoria died, when both world wars were fought, when England won the World Cup, when Apollo 11 landed on the moon?

—

When I next had Jasmine, I told her about what I'd found over breakfast. I'd noticed she had been getting more upset at hand-overs lately. Every time she drove away in her mother's car, a tearful hand on the window, it was as if the crushing awfulness of the breakup happened all over again, for all three of us, replayed in fast-forward. So, I came up with a variety of strategies that I hoped would ease the anxiety of her double life. There was the book *Two Homes*, and movies like *Finding Nemo* and *Toy Story*, which are both about coping with change and finding new ways to be happy. We discussed her mother a lot, which wasn't always a picnic, especially when Jasmine talked so glowingly about her mother's new ice cream-dispensing boyfriend.

I also wanted to turn the house into something she looked forward to coming home to. This began with spending the equivalent of Mr Tumble's quarterly tax bill on bedroom accoutrements – a beanbag, a teepee, fairy lights, a pink IKEA wardrobe. But this strategy needed more than just stuff to see it through. It needed a narrative. So, I tried to create a world with stories that I hoped, like all childhoods, would glue hers together.

'Remember how I told you about the moon, Jasmine?' I started, reminding her of our little ritual for when we were apart. 'And how whenever you miss me, you can look at it and know I'm looking at the same moon?'

She nodded, a spoonful of Rice Krispies halfway to her mouth. 'Well, I think there used to be a girl a bit like you who lived here and looked out through the window at the stars. I found a secret message from her.'

Jasmine's eyes saucered. 'What did it say?' she said, forgetting her mouth was full, so milk and cereal dribbled down her chin and onto Bunny, on her lap.

'She wrote her name next to a heart.'

She wrinkled her nose. 'Why?'

'I don't know,' I said, realising I would have to work harder to stick this landing. 'Maybe she liked him. Like a prince.'

Now this, to a little girl raised on an almost exclusive cultural diet of heteronormative princesses and talking animals, was the golden-buzzer answer. After a huge and wondrous intake of breath, she exhaled, 'Like Wapunzel?'

'Yeah, yeah, like Rapunzel. And I think she used to look out at the stars, like we do, and think about him.'

For about three full minutes, she lapped this up, wanting to know everything about the girl at the window. How old was she? Did she have sisters? Did she marry the prince? Did they have kids? Where do they live now? Do they have a dog? When she ran out of questions, she frowned.

'Daddy,' she said, 'will people live here after us?'

'Probably,' I said. 'And they'll wonder about us, just like we're wondering about the people who lived here before.'

'Will they find my toys?' she asked, clutching Bunny by the ear.

'Maybe they'll find a little teddy bear hidden in the attic,' I said, 'and imagine the little girl who loved it very much.'

Now she was shining, shining at me, dazzled by the magic of time and the world and her place in it. 'Can we do a secret message in my bedroom for them?'

'That's a great idea,' I said. 'We can make our own mark on this house, so that a part of us will always . . .'

Before I could finish, she had climbed down from her chair and grabbed a green felt-tip from the pen pot. She was heading for the stairs.

'Er, where are you going?' I demanded.

'To my bedroom.'

'Whatever you do,' I said sternly, 'please do not draw on the walls.'

—

By the afternoon, with Jasmine at school, I was back in the dusty attic at Walthamstow's Vestry House, surrounded by old maps, leather-bound books and newspapers. This was where the borough tucks away its archive office – a goldmine for anyone who cares lots about town-hall minutes and civic data, and not much about time. Apart from the clerk, the only other person in there that day was a gloriously fat man with lunch on his T-shirt, who spent the whole time with his head buried in the microfiche reader.

Incidentally, if anywhere in Walthamstow should be haunted, it is Vestry House. For more than a hundred years, it was a workhouse where local destitutes did hard labour, from digging roads to the classically soul-destroying Victorian punishment of unpicking old rope to make glue for ships. You can still read its judderingly biblical motto on a plaque above the door: *If any would not work, neither should he eat.* The building was later turned into a police station, then an armoury, then a private house. As you'd expect with a building of such vintage, it is powerfully creepy in places, especially the old prison cell, where two peeling waxworks leer through the bars like drunk ghosts. I would not like to spend the night alone at Vestry House.

Anyway, I was there to exhume the names buried in my own house's past. And I had come to the right place. By strict appointment, you can look at old maps of the borough, read old newspapers on microfilm, check electoral rolls by year, view census records, read birth, marriage and death notices, and so on. The volunteers who worked there were very helpful and attentive, and completely uninterested in why I was so concerned by a single address. They gave me what I needed and left me to tumble down a rabbit hole of forgotten names and lost jobs, dusty newspapers and birth records.

I entered that attic in search of the dead, and I emerged with a notepad teeming with life.

Chapter 21

THE POWER OF THE PAST

The first resident of the patch of land where my house now stands was most likely a cow. Or possibly a family of turnips. That was before the factories and tram stops, the train lines and churches, plane trees and pubs. Before all of that, it was a small square in a quilt of fields. My particular field was bordered by dry-stone walls, with a farmhouse at the top of the hill and a brook at the bottom. Old Victorian maps show a gravel pit a hundred yards to the east, and a pond where cattle drank to the north.

My house was built in the year of Jack the Ripper, on the fringe of a city in the grip of a housing crisis. London in 1888 was a place of vivid inequality where the rich bathed in the petalled waters of empire and the poor swirled down the plughole. It was a place where decadent townhouses bordered abject slums, the stench of open sewers mingled with the whiff of cigars, and where the homeless commonly washed their lice-infested clothes in public fountains in the shadows of stone admirals and kings.

For working-class Londoners, the risk of destitution was never more than one misfortune away. Rents were rising, and long-term lodgings were difficult to find. Swathes of low-income housing stock had been demolished to make way for the railway boom and glitzy new boulevards such as Shaftesbury Avenue and Oxford

Street. Ever-larger numbers were funnelled into densely packed slums where crime, vice and unscrupulous landlords flourished. Social activists – such as Walthamstow's own William Morris – gave rousing speeches to vast crowds. Lawmakers agreed urgent action was needed. So, as London grew rich, it grew out. Rows of identical, hastily built terraces crept outwards, swallowing fields and villages in their wake: Croydon, West Ham, Tooting, Tottenham, Harlesden, Hendon, Hornsey. Once populated only by townsfolk and market gardens, these ancient settlements were soon overrun by London's marching army of bricks and mortar. By the late 1880s, it was Walthamstow's turn.

—

My house's plot was bought in the mid-1880s by a speculative building company for somewhere between £7 and £12 an acre (£600 to £1,000 today).[1] Among hundreds of others on this plot, my house was constructed by moustached men in hobnail boots and calico waistcoats. They shipped its timber skeleton from the Baltic states – sturdy pine and spruce torn from distant forests and carried across the North Sea by sailing ships. Its custard-yellow bricks were baked with Thames clay, ash and sand, and trucked in on carts drawn by mighty dray horses.

Every house on the street looked identical: two floors; downstairs for living, cooking, eating; upstairs for sleeping. Each had two chimney stacks, front and back, its silhouette rising against the smoky London sky like battlements. Fireplaces were installed on both levels to fight off the damp and chill. A small garden at the back offered a space to grow vegetables, hang washing and pop to the privy – a small shed with a wooden seat over a bucket. At the front, each house had a bay window, those elegant Victorian curves of glass and plaster, designed to flood front rooms with sunshine. The plot was bought by a company called the Eastern Counties Estates Exchange, who sold off individual houses at auctions held at The Elms pub in nearby Leytonstone.[2]

THE PACKERS[3] (1888–1894)

Spring, 1888. The sky is blue and endless, stretching over Walthamstow and away towards the smoky haze of central London. The air is different here. It's not clogged by soot and smells of effluent, but fresh with damp earth, dewy fields and paint. The street bustles with carts carrying the belongings of incoming families, up from London. Newlyweds John and Eliza Packer are standing outside my house, beside a newly planted sycamore sapling. They are the exact same age as I am when I move here 136 years later. Inside, there are no voices. No echoes of anyone, or anything. The house is bursting with emptiness – naked, newborn and ready for life. No one has ever cooked in its kitchen, or sat and read books in its living room, or made love in its bedroom. No one has properly belly-laughed here, or wept, or had a blazing row. No human has opened their eyes for the first time here, nor closed them for the last. These things will all happen. *All in good time.*

THE SPARKS (1895–1900)

By 1895, the Spark family have moved in from Islington. The head of the household is William, a thirty-three-year-old electrical engineer's clerk. He and his wife Eliza will live here for five years with their three daughters: Ellen, eleven; Florence, nine; and Ada, seven. They'll then move to a similar-sized house around the corner and finally have a son, William, the following year.

THE BOOTS (1901–1910)

By Queen Victoria's death, Jethro and Louisa Boot have moved in. They run a shoe shop on Markhouse Road and have brought their two youngest, Lottie, twenty-three, and eleven-year-old Rose. Their other five children have all left home for jobs as domestic servants or cooks or railway workers and have families of their own. Jethro, sixty, is a 'cordwainer' by trade, making boots from fresh leather. I imagine him drying cow hides on lines in the garden when space is short in his workshop. The house stinks of it, which the children make fun of, but, deep down, they like it. Whenever they smell leather, it reminds them of home.

Now, as I look about the living room, it crackles to life with the silent echoes of Boot family Christmases. The clinks of cutlery on plate, the laughter, the squeals of young children . . . All that's forgotten. They're all dead now, no longer able to tell the story of a house that tells a story about them. Still, when I think about their lives, I see their silhouettes cast silent shapes across my walls.

I think Louisa died here.

THE CUTTERS (1910–1915)

When the First World War breaks out, a marvellously appointed 'cutter of fancy materials' named Edward lives here with his wife,

Florence, and three young children: Edward, eight; Gladys, five; and Lawrence, three. I think of little Gladys Cutter especially, who was exactly Jasmine's age when she lived in the house. Was she unable to sleep without a beloved cuddly-toy animal? I wonder if she, like Jasmine, whispered secret wishes into the fireplace, hoping they would float up our chimney and come true.

THE PLUMBERS (1916–1932)

By the time the war ends, a plumber called William moves in with his wife, Elizabeth, and their children: Elizabeth, twelve; William, ten; and Leonard, three.

There's no record of anyone else living here for the next fifteen years. Reading between the lines, the Plumbers are likely followed by a succession of tenants, who possibly didn't vote and therefore leave no official record of their existence. By 1932, a new family have made this their home. They will stay here for the next thirty-seven years.

THE POSTONS (1932–1969)

Sunday 3 September 1939. 11.15 a.m. Christopher and Elizabeth Poston, also exactly my age, sit in the front room – they call it 'the parlour' now – huddled around the wireless. Their sons, Eric, seventeen, and Terrence, thirteen, are there too.

Their house looks very different from when the Boot family squeezed in here. The walls are papered in a fashionable geometric print, perhaps a repeating trellis or small bouquets. There's a gramophone on a sideboard and crocheted doilies on the armchair.

On the mantelpiece, a row of framed family photos stands beside a small vase of wildflowers picked from the marshes. In the back room, Louisa Boot's old Victorian stove is long gone, replaced by a freestanding cooker with a small oven, a Belfast sink with a draining board, and some small cupboards. The toilet is still outside.

The wireless crackles with the clipped syllables of Prime Minister Neville Chamberlain announcing that Britain is at war with Germany.

When the war ended, there was a street party to celebrate. Then another in 1953, for Queen Elizabeth II's Coronation. I found photos of these on a community Facebook group: the makeshift table stretching all the way along the street, the Union Jack cone-hats, triangle flags, 'coronation chicken' sandwiches, the huge smiles. Every house is festooned with bunting. One picture taken that day shows eight young women standing in a row with their arms round each other's waists. They're all wearing collared dresses with long skirts and frilly aprons, laughing. How beautiful and happy they all look. Might one of them be Elizabeth Poston?

—

The Packers. The Sparks. The Boots. The Cutters. The Plumbers. The Postons. How I wanted to reinvent their lives, give them opinions and desires and pull them from the mist. I wanted to know everything about them: what songs they whistled while washing the dishes, what they argued about over Sunday lunch, how they took their eggs. Did they believe unquestioningly in God, or keep a secret stash of gin behind the baked beans? Did they love this house, or curse its cramped rooms and squeaky floors?

Even though I am not related to any of these people, and the minutiae of their day-to-day lives are as distant from mine as mine are from the E17 Night Stalker, I felt a connection to them. I know the contours of this house, just as they did. I know its nooks and cracks, wrinkles and peccadillos – that creaky third step, the draft in the hallway, the way the light falls into the living room at dusk. Every autumn I sweep the same doorstep clean of leaves fallen from the same sycamore outside. Every spring, I pull weeds from the same ground in the garden. As I look out over London from the bedroom window, I see a very different skyline, but the same view.

THE SMITHS, THE ALDERMANS, THE IQBALS, KHANS, WHITES, LUCJAS, KUMARS, PATELS, ETC . . . (1969–2016)

After the Postons there were the Smiths, who had a son while living here through the 1970s. Then the Aldermans, who had none. I believe that in the 1980s the house passed between a succession of landlords. The electoral role shows a Babel of different names – Polish, Arabic, Hindu, English – nothing long-term. Some years were a complete blank. My guess is that this is when the bay window was torn out, the stairs were flipped, the downstairs dividing wall was knocked down – all original features that the house's early inhabitants would have valued. Landlords, who possibly never even visited, seemed to have turned the house into a commodity, its soul secondary to its yield.

As the 2000s rolled by, many more short-term tenants passed through with increasing frequency. I spent weeks trawling the electoral roll and social media for people who had lived in my house. I sent dozens of cold messages on Facebook and Instagram to strangers all over the world whose names matched ones I'd found linked to the house. Most didn't reply, and those who did claimed ignorance: *Sorry, you've got the wrong Angela, I've never lived in Walthamstow* or *Yes, I briefly lived in Walthamstow but I can't remember the name of the street.* Most frustratingly of all, I never found Suhanee – there was no record of her ever living here. Presumably because she was too young to vote. Like Vyas and all the others, she was a ghost. The only traces of her existence here were a few scratches on wood.

It was as if, from sometime in the 1990s, the house turned into one of those old weathered shells you see in wildlife documentaries, lying empty on the seabed; the mollusc that made its beautiful spiral whorls and pearly sheen has long since died, leaving it for passing hermit crabs to inhabit for a while until something better washes up. Then, when they're done, they throw it back to the mercy of the currents.

In a way, if anything, I was beginning to feel sorry for the very old shell that was my house – this tired old man with creaking bones and sagging skin. Perhaps all he needed was a little love and care, some joint surgery and a facelift.

I just wasn't sure where to start. Then, serendipitously, I was introduced to a couple named Bruno and Mathilde, whose home in West London had a past so dark it made mine look like Green Gables at Christmas.

Chapter 22

DENNIS'S HOUSE

195 Melrose Avenue is, as your friendly local estate agent might tell you, a 'lovingly appointed family home in a much sought-after location'. Nestled in leafy Cricklewood, West London, its neon-pink-painted door pops against its pristine-white facade. Two generous bay windows overlook a neatly paved front garden. A slate-tiled canopy overhangs the front door so residents can open an umbrella drily, before stepping out into the rain. It is as charming a place as you could hope to find in London. It does not look at all like a house where a dozen men were murdered and left to rot beneath the floorboards.

Nobody knows exactly how many young men Dennis Nilsen killed here between 1978 and 1981. Only four have been identified – Kenneth Ockendon, Martyn Duffey, Billy Sutherland and Malcolm Barlow. Not even Nilsen remembered the names of the others, just a hazy number. He would pick them up in pubs or on the street and lure them to his home on the promise of booze, sex or a bed for the night. Then, when they were drunk and comfortable, he would strangle them unconscious and drown them in a bucket or the sink. He would lie in bed with their stiffening corpses or watch TV with them. Sometimes he posed them in armchairs or performed sex acts upon them. Then, when their usefulness expired, he hid them beneath the floorboards or under the kitchen sink to rot. That is, until the stench grew overwhelming. Then he burned what was left of them on bonfires in the garden. The neighbours never suspected a thing.

—

Four decades later, on a crisp December morning, I rang the electronic doorbell beside the pink front door and listened. I heard a muffle of child's laughter, then a scuffle of little feet. A woman's voice, slightly French, made a plea to put on wellies or they'd be late for ballet practice. Then, the door swung open and a tall, handsome man in his early forties appeared with a beaming smile. A little barefoot girl was clutching one of his legs. She was about four years old, wearing a blue tutu and holding a sparkly magic wand. Behind them appeared her mother, also smiling, and holding a child's wellington boot in each hand.

'Matt!' the man said with a faint Portuguese accent, offering his hand. 'Great to meet you. Come in, come in. You like coffee, don't you?'

I had heard about Bruno and Mathilde from a mutual acquaintance named Chris a few weeks earlier. 'You know,' Chris told me, 'if you want to compare notes with someone else who lives in a home with a dark past, you should speak to Bruno and Mathilde. They've lived in a famous murderer's house for years, and they seem to love it.'

It seemed incredible that anyone could live in one of Britain's most famous so-called 'murder houses' and not be affected by the memory on some level. Like me, had nobody told them about the house's past before making the deal? Chris said they loved it.

But what could they love? Were they murder ghouls with goat-skull tattoos and a sideline selling hand-stitched voodoo dolls on Etsy? Did they live by night, incanting spirits and throwing occult dinner parties with 'blood spatter' cocktails? Well, and I write this without a bat squeak of irony, they did not look like those kinds of people at all.

'I don't think you'll feel any creepy vibes here,' said Bruno, leading me through to the living area. 'We've done a lot of work to it. It's just not that kind of a place.'

Bruno and Mathilde came to London in the 2010s from Portugal and France respectively. They met through work – both are in healthcare – and fell in love. Soon, they had saved enough money for a deposit. Cricklewood ticked all the right boxes – a quiet neighbourhood with good transport links and plenty of nearby green space. So, when the downstairs flat at 195 Melrose Avenue came on the market in 2016, it seemed the perfect ball of clay to mould around their dreams.

'It was on at a good price, and I can remember looking around and just thinking, "This place is not particularly nice, but it has so much potential,"' said Bruno. Then he grinned, 'As you English like to say, it was a proper fixer-upper.'

They were so taken by the property that they did not notice the estate agent's oddly off-kilter manner during the viewing. Then he pulled Bruno to one side. 'He asked if I had Googled the property,' recalled Bruno. 'That seemed a strange question to ask at a house viewing. I said I hadn't, and he said, "I recommend that you Google it before making any decisions."'

You don't ever want the place you've just fallen in love with to be plastered all over the internet as 'one of the most notorious houses in London'. But Bruno wasn't fazed. 'Sure, I was surprised when I looked up the address, and I know other buyers pulled out because of it, but it didn't change my initial impression of the flat,' he said, opening a large white floor-to-ceiling cupboard with a state-of-the-art coffee machine inside. 'It was perfect for our needs.'

With the help of Bruno's architect sister, he and Mathilde embarked on a complete makeover, knocking down internal walls to remodel the entire floorplan. Where Nilsen once slept, they configured a modern, open-plan living area with a bright extension and large sliding patio door that flooded the space with sunlight. Where Nilsen cooked, they built a home office with a view of the garden. Where Nilsen hid his victims' bodies, they poured concrete insulation beneath fresh pine flooring. They also added a second bathroom and a stylish new kitchen with custom-made cabinets imported from Portugal. Where Nilsen murdered guests, they slept: his living room became their bedroom, which was spacious and bright, with a neatly made bed at the centre and ice-white closets built into the wall.

Do they ever get true-crime rubberneckers knocking on the door, seeking to cop a feel of real horror? 'We occasionally get TikTokers filming and taking selfies outside, but not often, and they're not much trouble,' Bruno said.

There was a small spike in interest when ITV broadcast *Des*, a three-part drama starring David Tennant as Nilsen, in 2020. And if you're wondering, as I was: yes, Bruno and Mathilde did watch it; and no, they did not find it any more harrowing than a regular viewer might. 'The producers came to the flat to get a sense of where he lived, but in the end the set on the show didn't look anything like ours, plus it was mostly set at Nilsen's other address at Cranley Gardens in Muswell Hill.'

Bruno describes himself as a 'science guy', which under no circumstances should be misheard as with 'seance guy'. As a nurse, he deals in life and death and is trained to always seek the truth through empirical observation. So, for him, if anything happens to people when they spend time in places with horrific pasts, it happens only inside their heads. 'It's about what you believe,' he said. 'We all have our ways of coping and I'll always respect how other people experience the world. But the paranormal is not for me.'

He frothed some milk with a hiss of the coffee machine's steam wand. Then he added, 'If a light flickers, you should check the fuse box.'

We took our coffees to the sofa, which looked out onto the large garden where Nilsen built fires to burn his victims' bodies. (He only started flushing them down the toilet at his next address, in Muswell Hill, which is how he was ultimately caught). Bruno went over to the sliding patio door and opened it. 'Listen to that,' he said, before closing it in a way that reminded me of the balcony-door scene in *Ace Ventura: Pet Detective*. 'Can you hear it?'

'Hear what?' I said. 'I can't hear anything.'

'Exactly,' he said. 'The silence. Isn't it beautiful? How many places in London can you go where it is so quiet?'

My own place came to mind, but I didn't mention it. He had a point. The silence was, by London standards at least, practically Stygian.

'I love it,' he added. 'I sit in the lounge and I drink a coffee and I look outside. It's quiet. I can hear the birds. I have squirrels. There's a fox that pops by.'

As he said that, I heard a noise – the muffled sound of footsteps above our heads, then a bump. Bruno must have seen my eyes dart upwards because he laughed. 'Don't worry, it's not a ghost. We've got friends staying upstairs.'

In fact, the couple can have as many friends to stay as they like now – and often do – because, in 2022, they bought the top flat too. 'When it came onto the market, it seemed a no-brainer,' said Bruno, sinking back into the sofa and crossing his legs. 'We worked out a way to afford it, and it seemed the ideal opportunity to bring the two flats together into one house.' They now have five bedrooms, four bathrooms, two living rooms and two kitchens. And, with friends and family from all over the world, entertaining guests has become something of a family forte.

Has any of their guests ever felt the weight of the past? *No.* The couple says not one visitor has ever – ever! – complained of a strange atmosphere or heard bumps in the night or run into the street clutching their baby. 'What about your daughter?' I asked, half expecting him to reply, 'Daughter? We don't have a daughter!' But he didn't. 'She loves it here,' he said.

The floors do not creak, the shower does not leak, and the rooms are all as warm or as cool as the thermostat directs them. And, as Bruno showed me about the flat, I must say, hand on beating heart, I had no discernible physical response to the place, either.

I did not feel a shiver when we stepped into their bedroom where, on 3 December 1979, Nilsen garrotted twenty-three-year-old Kenneth Ockendon with a headphone cable as he listened to music, dragging him across the floor until life left his body.

No cold hand touched my shoulder in the living room, where Nilsen strangled fourteen-year-old Stephen Holmes with a necktie before drowning him in a bucket of water on 30 December 1978; and then sixteen-year-old Martyn Duffey eighteen months later, as well as up to ten other, never-identified, young men.

And, honestly, I did not get any creeps of any kind in the bathroom, where Nilsen bathed with the bodies of his victims before taking them to bed. It is now a walk-in shower tiled chicly in slate.

But then, I did not have to sleep there. I have never – and will never – get to wake up there in the middle of the night and listen to the silence, feel how steadily it lies, see if it cracks.

'Are you really not at all bothered by what happened here?' I said, taking a last gulp of white Americano.

'Look,' said Bruno, with serious eyes. 'It's not that we don't care what happened. What happened here was awful, unspeakable. The man was utterly evil and I cannot imagine what it must have been like for those poor men in their final moments. I am very sorry for them, and for their families, especially the ones who never found out what happened to their sons.'

He looked out of the sliding doors at the sky, where rain clouds were gathering. Then he said, 'But it was forty years ago. I can't change what happened. I can't control the past any more than I can control the weather. But I can control the future. Our future. Our daughter's future. We're not going anywhere. Not even if we won the lottery.'

Just then, we heard the front door open and the little girl in the tutu ran in and jumped on her father and hugged him. The wand was gone from her hand, replaced by a lollipop. Mathilde was behind her.

'How was ballet?' Bruno asked.

'Good,' said the girl in that matter-of-fact way young children do. 'But Daddy . . .' She tugged at his trouser.

'Yes, my love?'

'Can you make a cake with me today?'

Bruno stood up, scooping his daughter into his arms and plonking her onto his hip. 'Of course. Let's go and see if we have all the ingredients.'

As they rummaged about in those spacious Portuguese cupboards, Mathilde took off her coat. 'How about you?' I asked as I put mine on. 'Do you feel anything about living here, given what happened?'

She smiled kindly. 'I basically agree with Bruno, but maybe I have a slightly more diverse vision,' she said. 'Like, I know you said you have been going through a divorce and that must have been difficult, and I can absolutely imagine if your mind is in a certain place, knowing about a dark past might affect you. The brain is a powerful thing. It can play tricks. It can scare you.'

She stooped to pick up a soft toy their daughter had left on the floor. 'I think we have always been in a good place as a family, in our lives,' she said. 'The house has been good to us. We have transformed it into something we love, and when people come round we do everything we can to make them feel at home, to make them feel good.'

I thanked her for rolling out the red carpet for me. Then Bruno poked his head out from behind a kitchen cupboard door. 'It's really just the old glass-half-full or half-empty thing,' he said. 'However you choose to see it, it's the same bloody glass.'

I turned back to Mathilde. 'What about when Bruno is away? When you're alone in the house, and it's quiet and dark. Do you ever feel anything then?'

She thought for a moment. 'I hardly ever think about the past of this house,' she said. 'It's very sad, but it was in the past.'

She paused again. Then she said, 'Although, I probably wouldn't watch a horror movie on my own here. It just ... It might spark my imagination, and I'd rather not send my mind into that place.'

—

All this talk of horror movies got me thinking about Freddy Krueger, the knife-fingered dream monster of the *Nightmare on Elm Street* franchise. I thought about him all the way home. He is most powerful in the dream world. That's where he gets you, in the shadows that lurk in the dankest corners of your imagination. But bring him into the light, face him in the real world, and he becomes impotent – just an ugly old twat with a cutlery set stuck to a glove.

Could that be true of 'haunted' houses? For Bruno and Mathilde, the real horror of a house's awful history doesn't lie in creaking floorboards or flickering lights, but in the stories we tell ourselves, and have been told since we were small. It is one of the great dramas of human identity that indoor spaces can elicit such varied and extreme feelings in us. A prison cell doesn't feel the same as a broom closet. A church isn't like a cinema. One man's ghost-plagued Gothic mansion teetering over a Transylvanian cliff edge is another man's romantic weekend getaway. For them, Nilsen's shadow is no more than a culture-induced hallucination.

Don't doubt it: 195 Melrose Avenue has about as sickening a history as a building can have. And yet, whatever cracks there once were in its *genius loci* seemed to have been caulked and Polyfilla'd, sanded and painted over with laughter, love and the pitter-patter of welly-less feet. Whatever darkness once walked there had, it seemed, long since walked away.

I thought for a long time about the last thing Bruno said to me when I left his house: 'We can choose to live in fear, or we can choose to face our fears. The space is yours. Reclaim it with your own stories.'

Chapter 23

THE PURGE

I should have foreseen what was coming. The flies had been trying to tell me all along. As their numbers increased, their buzzing grew louder, rasping around the house like a broken telephone. They crawled across windows, on indoor plants, over surfaces. If you stepped away from the table to grab the ketchup from the fridge, you'd come back to find one picking through your food. I'd swatted so many that killing them had turned into sport. Even Jasmine joined in on the game, chasing flies with the swatter before presenting their squished carcasses to me in her palm like a proud kitten with a mouse.

I finally got the flies' message on the day I threw my first party.

'I'm going to throw a party,' I told Jody over the phone. 'Nothing massive, just a few people. Call it a gathering, a friends' convention.'

'A party,' she said. 'That's not like you.'

'I know, but I think it'll do me good. I need something to look forward to, to take my mind off this house for a bit.'

'You mean it'll do the house good, don't you?' she said with a smile in her voice. 'You want to throw a party for the house.'

She was right. I had spent the weeks since The Night of the

Rat trying not to think about the house as a living thing, or about Vyas or about the sewer below ground.

On the nights I didn't have Jasmine with me, I made a point of staying at Jody's, so I didn't have to be at home by myself. I had stopped working at home too, commuting to the British Library every day instead.

But I knew I couldn't live like this forever. I was determined to at least test Bruno's theory about reclaiming spaces with stories. A party could be the prologue; a good-vibe transfusion. So, I chose a Saturday evening when Jasmine would be with Lisa, created a WhatsApp group titled 'House Whisperers', and invited all my funniest friends.

When the day came, I spent the morning in a rubber-gloved cleaning frenzy. That's when I caught it: a stench that crawled so far up my nose that I almost felt it in my eyes. I had grown accustomed to smells in the house by now. They still came and went, but I had given up trying to locate their sources. I was getting through a can of Oust a week, on top of enough scented candles to start a new religion. But this smell sliced through it all.

This wasn't drains or damp. It was worse than the worst morning breath I'd ever smelled; worse than fox shit worked into dog fur; worse than vomit on a train seat. It smelled like all those things, mixed with bin juice, fetid vase water and spilled milk left to sour under a fridge. There was something vaguely fruity to it too. But these are just words. Death is a smell unto itself. It really was as if the house were putrefying from the inside out. Only this time it was locatable.

I followed my nose into the kitchen. It was strongest in the corner, around the counter where I kept the bread bin. But it wasn't that. It was coming from under the cabinet. I crouched down, peering into the shadows beneath the sink. Nothing. Then, I noticed a tiny gap where the kickboard had come loose. With rising dread, I fetched a screwdriver and prised it off completely.

There she was. She had her back to me, but it had to be her. That browny-grey fur, the snaking tail. She was moving, but not of her own accord. Maggots writhed in her open mouth, wriggled out of her eye sockets and crawled across her distended belly. A few flies skittered about the carcass like newborn minions ready to fly. I fell backwards, gagging. Could this really be the same rat? She seemed larger, but it was hard to tell through the teeming mass of maggots. The rat-catcher's words came back to me: 'Maggots will eat through the carcass of a rat in days . . .' *Days.* This thing had been rotting beside my feet since at least Tuesday, I guessed. Maybe longer.

Guests would be arriving in a few hours. With trembling hands, I grabbed a broom handle and, holding my breath, nudged the carcass out onto the kitchen floor. It stuck for a moment, then dislodged with a squelch. As it came loose, a leg detached and remained stuck to the underside of the cabinet. I gagged again.

I could see some ribs, and maggots had made light work of her face, exposing a row of sharp teeth to look like a hideous smile. Her eyes were no longer beady and black, but crawling sockets. I scooped her up with the dustpan and dropped the carcass into a plastic bag. Before I tied the bag and binned it, I took one last look at her. Had the rat flap in the sewer jammed? Rather than do its job, it must have trapped this rat in the house, leaving her no choice but to make a home here, alongside us.

I almost felt sorry for her. She had only set out for shelter and a bite to eat. Perhaps she was looking for somewhere safe and warm to raise some young. But in all the homes in all of Walthamstow, she chose this house of horrors. She probably thought she had struck gold at first – all those little trays of delicious green grains doused in sweet-smelling toxins that liquify your insides. Slowly she got sick. Then, as her organs failed one by one, she curled up in this dark corner of the kitchen and let the poison do its work.

Perhaps we had something in common after all, she and I.

—

'So, are you the rat?' said Nick when I told him this at the party that evening. 'You're the rat, and the E17 Night Stalker is the poison? What's the house?'

'The house is the house, or maybe it's the poison,' I said over the hubbub. 'It's an allegory, Nick. Come on, you must admit it's kind of poignant.'

He dipped a chip in the guacamole on the table and popped it into his mouth. 'Seriously,' he said visibly unseriously. 'You need to lay off the Kafka, mate. Before you start waking up with whiskers and a craving for cheese.'

He laughed, put his hands out in front of his face as if reading a billboard, and said grandly, '*The Mattamorphosis.*'

In the end, about fifteen people came to the party, though it felt like fifty by the way we filled the downstairs space. It was joyful to see the house so alive, so loud. Even as I cleared away the cans and wine bottles and half-eaten bowls of Doritos the next morning, I felt a change in the way the air hung. Lighter, fresher. Of course, nothing *had* changed. The shower had awoken me at 3 a.m. only two nights before. The cold spot on the stairs hadn't warmed. But I could feel something happening. Perhaps the change was in me.

—

I never did hear back from the parish priest I'd emailed about deliverance services. It had been months since I'd sent it, plus a follow-up email. I did ask a churchgoing friend who said he didn't think all priests go in for that side of things.

'I think deliverance is most effective when you believe it can work,' he said.

'Sounds like reiki,' I said.

'What it sounds like is religion,' he replied. 'In the absence of rock-solid physical evidence, it comes down to what you *choose* to believe.'

Well, thanks. But this wasn't a question I was ready to put to God. If it is about belief, then what did I believe caused these things to happen in my house? Well, it wasn't ghosts. It was never about ghosts. At least, not the kind some people see. But there was a haunting in this house, something mean and insidious that was dragging me towards darkness.

A few weeks before his own death, Einstein wrote a moving condolence letter to the family of a recently deceased friend. In it, he told them that 'the distinction between the past, present and the future is only a stubbornly persistent illusion'.[1] Or, as any philosophy student who's loitered long enough in the faculty toilets to read the graffiti knows: 'Time exists so that everything doesn't happen all at once . . . Space exists so it doesn't all happen to you.'[2]

Was the house haunted by the accumulated horrors of its past

– the murderous rapist, the fires, the succession of drifters passing through? Cannabis farms are famously miserable places, often disguised in terraced houses and inhabited by trafficked slaves held captive by drug gangs. As Pamela Heath said, 'Your house would have awful place memory . . . just awful.' Even Dean Radin, the physicist, entertained the hypothesis that I was picking up some quantum 'echo from the past' – that Vyas, a man of such lascivious emotional intensity that it drove him to murder, had left a black energy that soaked into the walls like smoke.

Or what if I was suffering from long-term exposure to Vyas's own molecular residue? That the house literally absorbed molecules emanating from his body – his self-loathing, his libidinous urges; you name it – that I had been inhaling this whole time. 'I'll buy that at the most intuitive level,' said Noam Sobel, the neurobiologist. My olfactory response to the house may not have stopped there. The strange smells, the pernicious whiffs of death and fire, certainly contributed to my experience of the space.

Or was it the house itself – a sickness of the very ground on which it stood? The sewer below was certainly, for a while, a rodent gateway. Could it also have disrupted the electromagnetic equilibrium of the land, and then my mind? Well, Gerhard Hacker said geopathic stress can cause all manner of ailments, especially disrupted sleep.

All of this, or just some, may have contributed to my deteriorating sense of self in the house. The sickness and sadness I felt. It may even have explained the infestations, as if some undetectable energy had stirred them up. But it didn't explain the weird events that happened here – the cold spots, the phantom radio, the late-night doorbell, the ghost shower.

Were they all merely coincidences, as Alastair Wilson suggested? A conspiracy of unsourceable anomalies, each born from the chaos of an uncaring universe where the tiniest actions ripple through time and space to create unforeseen consequences. Did I connect dots that weren't there?

There is one last possibility: that the house was never haunted at all. Rather, it was me. Haunted by my own past, and by the past of this house, my anxiety took on a life of its own, turning the building into a mirror for my inner turmoil – my Freudian 'id' gone rogue to force me to confront the wolf growing inside me. Months later, I emailed Pamela about the night of the spooky coin. 'The dropping coin has been reported in multiple poltergeist cases,' she wrote back. 'If it's your unconscious, see whether you can figure out the message it's trying to give you and incorporate psi into your life in a healthy/useful way. Fear and anxiety aren't it. Think of it as fun and entertaining instead.'

—

Now, even when it's cold and the moon is out, I'll still tell you I don't believe in ghosts. But I will buy any one of these explanations. Or even a random confluence of them all. Real or imagined, Vyas *did* leave something of himself behind here. Whether it was something physical, indistinct or just an unexpected plot twist in a narrative I was building, his memory stalked this house. *In the absence of rock-solid physical evidence, it all comes down to what you choose to believe.*

But there's something else, isn't there? Control. Like Bruno said, we can't control the past any more than we can control the weather. But we can buy an umbrella. I knew I needed to reclaim my life, my sanity, my home. And the only way to do that, I resolved, was to act.

So, in January 2022, a year after I bought this house, I launched the purge. No holy water, no invocations, no magic crystals. Just hammers and drills and a skip. Call it an exorcism of dust and sweat.

It wasn't about flushing out ghosts. It was about demolishing the remnants of Vyas's memory, and turning this house, this old conch, into a home. Every swing of the hammer would be a strike against his nagging presence, every ripped-up floorboard a step towards claiming this space as our own.

It was a sunny Saturday, a week after the party. Brisk but bright. Purge-perfect weather. It was obvious which room to start with. I'd already scraped off half the wallpaper in my bedroom. Anyway, it felt right to leave a few Mickey Mouses up there for future inhabitants to discover down the line. I entombed them behind a skim of plaster and three coats of a blue that floated between the Royal Navy and John Lee Hooker.

Next, the charred floorboards. I pulled up three of them myself before realising this was a job I had neither the conviction nor qualifications to do. So, I found a handyman called Mark, who arrived in a van so full of tools that it rattled when he parked. Two days later, I had a new pine floor that smelled of Norwegian forests.

The plan had always been to renovate. I had held back cash from the mortgage and had been saving up all year. So, I hired a building firm from Essex to convert my attic into a loft. They sent two young men called Gary and Ryan, who were friendly and hardworking and always brought their own teabags.

For the next three months, they pulled down old beams, inserted steel joists, drilled, banged and built until an en-suite bedroom took form.

—

Weeks passed, then months. The sycamore grew new leaves, pages flew from the calendar. I watched the house change. It wasn't just the loft – I had the peeling, syphilitic render at the front of the house chipped off and redone in 'monocouche'. I replaced the windows and installed a new front door in racing green.

In one costly but necessary addition to the work, the chief builder, Steve, told me we would have to return the staircase to its original position – facing front. 'This would never pass fire safety control as it is,' he told me. 'They'll have done this on the quiet.'

Funny, that, I thought.

Steve continued, 'There always needs to be a clear escape route out of the house that doesn't pass the kitchen. It's that, or you install a sprinkler system throughout the whole house.'

'How much are sprinklers?' I asked.

'Three grand.'

'Flip the stairs,' I said.

When that was done, I had new carpets installed in the bedrooms and painted the stairs and landing charcoal grey. Slowly, I brought in new furniture, too: a sofa in sage green, a mid-century G Plan sideboard from eBay, white-wood blinds. Spike helped me paint more walls in warm colours. Nick helped me build shelves for my books with cast-iron brackets and reclaimed scaffold planks. Even Michael from next door chipped in, helping me re-gutter the bay window and replace the rotting fascia and soffit boards in the roof. That spring, the rose shrub in the garden finally bloomed. Its petals are Barbie pink.

Chapter 24

HOME

I've got the sage!' came the text message, accompanied by a witch emoji. 'When is good to come round?'

It had been many months since Lisa had last been over – not since that day I told her about the house's past and she offered to smoke-cleanse it. For a long time since, relations had been frosty. But as the seasons warmed, so had we. We'd found a rhythm of childcare, and the handovers in select supermarket carparks had become . . . almost pleasant. More than that, something had shifted in me.

To make a baby might be the most profound thing two people can do together. Today, I am always bowled over when I hear of divorced parents, where abuse wasn't a factor, still unable to be in the same room after years apart. It seems so solipsistic, so craven, not to at least give post-marriage friendship a shot when kids are involved. It wasn't simple; Lisa and I worked hard to rebuild each other's trust. Many a phone was hung up in anger, many an eye-roll emoji regretted.

But the truth is, when the guns run out of ammo and the fog lifts, how can you resent the one person whose face you see every time you look into the eyes of the thing you love most in the world?

'How about next Saturday?' I wrote back.

'Yep,' she replied. 'Saturday's good.'

My phone buzzed again: 'Why don't we all go out for lunch after? Might be nice for Jazzy to see us all together. Jody, too???'

When Saturday came, Lisa arrived in a white satin shirt, jeans and red lipstick, holding a sheaf of sage bound in string. Jasmine was in the bathroom trying to wash the freckles off her face. But she bounded down the stairs when she heard her mother's voice. She launched herself into Lisa's arms, dripping wet flannel down her back.

'Oh, you're all wet!' Lisa said, her shoulders visibly tightening in cold shock. 'What have you been doing?'

Jasmine hugged tighter, burying her face in Lisa's neck. 'I missed you, Mummy!'

'I missed you too, darling,' said Lisa in a soft voice. Then she turned to me. 'I like what you've done to the place. Doesn't feel as gloomy as last time.'

'A work in progress,' I said. 'Still has its moments though.'

'Well, let's see if this can't make a difference,' she said brightly, putting Jasmine down before pulling a lighter out of her handbag and holding it to the sheaf.

Soon, white smoke began to billow, and the room filled with a smell somewhere between high-grade cannabis and sage-and-onion stuffing.

'So, are we smudging?' I asked.

'Well, no,' she said, waving smoke away from her face. 'Smudging is what Native Americans do. It involves burning sage, but other rituals as well. You have to be taught how to do that properly or it's considered cultural appropriation.'

'Oh, right,' I said. 'What are we doing, then?'

'We're smoke-cleansing. Here, you try.'

She handed me the sheaf and I held it at arm's length, twirling it in small, tentative circles.

'Come on, wave it about a bit,' said Lisa. 'Don't make that face, it won't bite. We want smoke to fill the whole space.'

So together, we stood in silence watching the smoke twist and swirl towards the ceiling, mushrooming on impact and peeling off about the room.

At that moment, Jasmine wrinkled her nose. 'Smells like sausages.'

'That's because they put sage in sausages,' said Jody, entering the room from upstairs. She waved smoke away from her face. 'She's right, though. It does smell sausagey.'

Lisa let out an easy laugh, replaced instantly by a look of panic as she stamped dramatically on the rug by my foot. It was the first time I'd seen Lisa and Jody in a room together and, in my distraction, I hadn't spotted the embers falling from the sage bundle onto the floor. Half a dozen of them were now glowing red among the fibres of my fancy new faux-wool Berber style rug. They were starting to smoke. They were threatening to send the whole thing up in flames.

'Oh shit!' Lisa yelped, grinding the embers with her boot. 'Sorry, sorry! Didn't realise it would drop bits.'

The dark irony of burning down the house now – after everything – wasn't lost on any of us. We exchanged nervous glances, a mix of amusement and relief. Maybe this house wasn't all out of surprises just yet.

'I think that'll do,' said Lisa. 'Now leave it and see. Who's hungry?'

'Me!' sang Jasmine. 'Can I have bangers and mash?'

As we stepped outside, Jody, Lisa and Jasmine walked over to the car. After weeks of heavy rain, the big sky was again bright blue, with high candyfloss clouds stretching towards the skyscrapers of central London. As I locked the front door, something caught my eye. A flash of yellow and electric blue. It was a blue tit, no bigger than Jasmine's fist, flittering about my roof. Yellow breast, black bandit mask, a twig hanging jauntily from its beak like a cigarette. In and out of the eaves it went, a frantic little architect on a deadline. It was building a nest. Right there, under the roof that had sheltered so much darkness, new life was beginning to stir.

—

Aman Vyas never did write back to me. I suppose I can understand why he might not want to talk to me. Perhaps, to him, this house meant nothing more than a pit stop, a bag drop, a weathered old shell to crawl into and hide. He might not even remember the name of the street. Or maybe, as the prison lights clunk out, he lies in his cell with nowhere to go but his thoughts, and they turn to his short stay in Walthamstow. I wonder what story he tells himself about that time.

I wrote to him because I thought he might shed light on the story of my house, that he might provide answers. But I realise now that there could be no light, no colour. Not from him. As a subject, Vyas drained away colour. He was – and will always be – just the sketch of a man in the shape of a crime, a puff of smoke rising off the ashes of the lives he destroyed. He will be remembered for nothing other than the terrible things he did.

—

A few weeks after Lisa's sage-burning ceremony, I was alone at home, cleaning. It was another bright-blue day and sunlight tumbled in with an almost magical energy. I vacuumed and sprayed and wiped and mopped until I could taste bleach in my throat and had dust in my eyes. When it came to Jasmine's bedroom, I pulled her bed away from the wall. As I swept the hoover head along the skirting board, I noticed a strange green mark. I crouched down for a closer look. It wasn't a mark; it was writing. A child's writing. It was Jasmine's writing in green felt-tip pen. She must have crawled under her bed to write this when I was in another room – perhaps that day I told her not to. At four years old, her writing wasn't perfect – she often got her 'd's mixed up with her 'b's and whether she chose to express herself in upper or lower case depended on a letter-by-letter lottery. But I could read this message clear as a premonition.

JAsmiNe

It was a message in a bottle without a bottle or an ocean. I was instantly transported back to that day she asked if the Big Bad Wolf could blow our home down, when I told her no: love can't be blown down. This was her declaration of existence, a felt-tip flag planted on the territory of her home.

I never asked her about it, and she never confessed. So, I left it there: a private conversation between her and our house.

Our house. If I'd known about its past from the beginning, would I have still bought it? Perhaps not. But this house has forced me to confront my own demons and think about what I really want from a home.

I am the twentieth owner of this house since it was built 137 years ago. Many more have called it 'home'. From the moment people first wandered into a cave, found it empty and lit a fire, we have built stories in and around the places in which we choose to live. I'm choosing *our* story. And I'm giving the E17 Night Stalker nothing more than a footnote.

—

It's said that an average person will walk past thirty-six murderers in their lifetime.[1] For all I know I brushed past Vyas himself one sunny day in the summer he lived in London back in 2008. I can't erase his memory from this house completely. But if it does still linger, I can choose to overwrite it, to ignore it. This is what I am determined to do.

So, now, when the shower turns itself on in the middle of the night, which it still does from time to time, when a shadow shifts in the corner of my eye, a door slams, or I feel a shiver on a stair, I remember that I am lucky to own a home at all. Then I check all the locks, turn out the lights and go back to bed.

Jasmine and I are beginning to find little pieces of happiness all over this house. It has become a place of so many firsts – her first day at school, her first new tooth, my first passive-aggressive Post-it note received under the door saying, 'Dear Daddy, I <u>hayt</u> you, Love Jasmine'. It's where we had our first solo Christmas together, and where I taught her to write her own name. I've stayed up all night with her in this house when she's been sick. It has kept me company when she's been asleep. Happy memories are piling up;

I think we'll stay happy here. But the truth is, although my name may be on the deeds of the property, I no longer feel as if we really own it. We just take care of it. And for now, it's taking care of us.

So, if you're reading this, years from now, because you're considering buying this house from me and you Googled my name . . . don't pull out or try to haggle on the price just because a murderer once lived here. He did. But so did we. I can't tell you how many times we've laughed in here or danced like maniacs to 2000s pop. How many fish-finger sandwiches we've gobbled down, cakes we've baked (and burned), or bathtimes we've had with bubble beards and mermaid toys.

So don't be frightened. Come on in. We've left a little something for you. Call it a housewarming gift. Sorry, it won't get you drunk or look nice in a vase. It's more of a feeling, really. But it's here, hidden all about the house; in the walls and on the air. I hope you find it. And when you do – if you do – remember: *this home was made of love; and love can't be blown down.*

The End

ACKNOWLEDGEMENTS

This book was born in the dark, in a quiet place, but it took a village of wonderful, clever and generous people to help me bring it into the light. Foremost, I must thank everyone who agreed to be in it, for sharing their time, wisdom and work, especially Steve Lynch, Shaleena Sheikh, Jason Bray, Christine Simmonds-Moore, Pamela Heath, Dean Radin, Alastair Wilson, Noam Sobel, Jasper de Groot, Carl Philpott and Gerhard Hacker. Thanks to Bruno, Mathilde and Natalie for inviting me into their homes, sharing their stories and showing me that a home doesn't just happen to you, but the other way around. Then there are the people who didn't know they were going to be in a book until it was too late. They are Michael and Jackie; my brothers Nick and Spike; Laura, Louis and, of course, Hector.

Converting experience into words is one thing, but words work best with someone else to tell you when you've used too many, or not enough, and to kill your darlings when you can't bear to pull the trigger yourself. For that I thank Katie Bond, Sarah Rigby, Pippa Crane, Amy Greaves and everyone else at E&T. Thanks for your trust, patience and the care you gave these pages.

There would be no book without many of the people on this page, but none more so than Dotti Irving, my fabulous agent. Thank you for your belief, support and boundless encouragement. And deep thanks to everyone else at Greyhound Literary, too.

C. S. Lewis wrote that friendship has no survival value; rather, it gives value to survival. I thank all my friends who listened patiently to me blathering on about this book and, before that, about the house and, before that, about my divorce. I'm lucky to know you. But there is one to whom I am most grateful: Morwenna Ferrier, who persuaded me to write the *Guardian* article on which this book is based and then edited it into something people wanted to read. Thanks for all the coffee, walks and words.

I also thank Joe Mackertich, Lucy Werner, Kate Murray-Browne, Laura Macaulay, Mark Wilding, J. S. Rafaeli, Guy Stevenson, Ben Schofield, Sam Hunt and Alex Miller for their time reading half-baked drafts of chapters, bouncing ideas and sharing thoughts. I'm grateful for the advice . . . especially what I took.

Thanks, too, to Fanny and Robin Blake for their love, and for teaching me that home is far more than just a place; it's people.

Thank you, Lisa, for being a wonderful mother to our daughter, and for allowing me to commit my interpretation of a painful part of both our lives to print.

Then, of course, there is Jody, who has been elemental to this journey. Thank you for shining on through the darkness, for remaining warm when it got cold, and for your ability to smell a rat when you hear one.

Finally, Jasmine. You are, in the words of another dear friend to whom I owe much, my arms and legs. I wouldn't work without you. And if you're reading this, then I guess you're old enough by now to understand. I hope you do.

ENDNOTES

Prologue
1. David Eagleman, 'The Umwelt', in *This Will Make You Smarter*, ed. John Brockman (Harper Perennial, 2012). Available at: https://eagleman.com/latest/umwelt/

Chapter 2
1. 'Council Tax: Stock of properties statistical commentary', Office for National Statistics, 21 September 2023

Chapter 3
1. 'Number of sexual offences in England and Wales: 2002–2024', Statista, 14 April 2025
2. 'Recorded rape up 53% in London', BBC News, 25 May 2012

Chapter 4
1. 'Homicide in England and Wales', Office for National Statistics, 2021–24, https://www.statista.com/statistics/283100/recorded-rape-offences-in-england-and-wales
2. 'Council Tax: Stock of properties statistical commentary', Office for National Statistics, 21 September 2023
3. 'Crime and income deprivation report, 2024', Trust for London, 2025
4. Sykes v Taylor-Rose, Court of Appeal, 27 February 2004

Chapter 5
1. Irving Finkel, *The First Ghosts* (Hachette, 2021)
2. 'How religious are British people?', YouGov, 29 December 2020
3. '"Ghosts exist", say 1 in 3 Brits', YouGov, 31 October 2014
4. 'Spirituality among Americans', Pew Research Center, 7 December 2023

5. Paul Brewer, 'Haunting messages: Online videos and public belief in paranormal phenomena', *Cyberpsychology, Behavior, and Social Networking*, 9 September 2024. Available at: https://www.liebertpub.com/doi/10.1089/cyber.2023.0667

6. This story is possibly apocryphal and may be a conflation of Churchill's famous naked encounter with Harry S. Truman and multiple alleged sightings of Lincoln's ghost at the White House. However, the Churchill scholar Richard Langman quotes a story from the *Baltimore Sun* ('Churchill's ersatz meeting with Lincoln's ghost', richardlangworth.com, 31 January 2018) that claimed the British statesman, 'who thought nothing of taking on Hitler and Mussolini, was not happy when assigned to the Lincoln Bedroom . . . Quite often, he was found in a vacant bedroom across the hall the next morning.' Churchill did, on multiple occasions, imply a belief in the paranormal, and is often quoted as saying, 'I believe that man is an immortal spirit.' The American historian Jon Meacham wrote in *Franklin and Winston* (Random House, 2003) that this prompted Churchill's final private secretary to label him an 'optimistic agnostic'. 'Whether you believe or disbelieve,' Meacham quotes Churchill as saying, 'it is a wicked thing to take away Man's hope.'

7. On 14 May 1930, just two months before his death, Sir Arthur Conan Doyle commercially released a speech on spiritualism on gramophone disc. In it, he discussed his experiences of speaking with the dead, which, he said, was possible 'beyond all doubt'. A copy of the speech survives at the British Library and can be heard in person or online via its 2014 blog article, 'The spirit voice of Sir Arthur Conan Doyle'. Even more hauntingly, you can also listen to a recording of Conan Doyle's alleged spirit voice, summoned at a public seance in 1934, four years after his death, before an audience of 560 paying guests. Available here: https://blogs.bl.uk/english-and-drama/2014/05/the-spirit-voice-of-sir-arthur-conan-doyle.html

8. Alan Turing, 'Computing machinery and intelligence', *Mind*, vol. 59 (1950)

9. Carl Jung, *Synchronicity: An Acausal Connecting Principle* (Routledge, 1955)

10. 'Aliens, God & Evolution – Richard Dawkins & Brian Greene', YouTube, uploaded by Pangburn, 29 November 2018. Available at: https://www.youtube.com/watch?v=7iQSJNI6zqI

Chapter 7

1. 'London police hunting killer rapist seek DNA from 9,000 homes', *Guardian*, 12 June 2009
2. Ibid.
3. 'Warning to women over suspected serial rapist', *Waltham Forest Guardian*, 9 June 2009
4. 'Killer "may have raped two more"', BBC News, 6 June 2009
5. *Crimewatch*, BBC, 4 July 2009. Available at: https://www.youtube.com/watch?v=rsTpy0WPwUA
6. 'Homicide victims in the MPS: 2003 to 2024', Metropolitan Police statistics. Available at: https://www.met.police.uk/sd/stats-and-data/met/homicide-dashboard/
7. 'Murder investigation into the death of Michelle Samaraweera continues one year on', *Waltham Forest Guardian*, 18 May 2010
8. 'Rape and murder suspect cannot be extradited', *The Times*, 4 March 2016
9. Hansard, HC (series 5) vol. 639, col. 324 (18 April 2018)
10. 'Indian fugitive charged after extradition to UK', *Hindustan Times*, 5 October 2019
11. R v Vyas, Croydon Crown Court, 20 August 2020
12. 'London murderer and serial rapist jailed for at least 37 years', *Guardian*, 20 August 2020

Chapter 8

1. 'The spirit attachment removal process', Dr. Wanda Pratnicka Center. Available at: https://wandapratnicka.com/services/the-spirit-attachment-removal-process/

Chapter 9

1. 'Safeguarding children, young people and vulnerable adults', Church of England Safeguarding Manual. Available at: https://www.churchofengland.org/safeguarding/safeguarding-e-manual/safeguarding-children-young-people-and-vulnerable-adults/4-1
2. 'Muslim family "haunted by monk" call priest for exorcism as "ghost was Christian"', *The Sun*, 20 January 2019
3. Jason Bray, *Deliverance* (Hachette, 2022)
4. 'Religion, England and Wales: Census 2021', Office for National Statistics, 2021

Chapter 10

1. Sue Townsend, *The Secret Diary of Adrian Mole Aged 13 ¾* (Methuen, 1982)
2. Oscar Wilde, 'The Canterville Ghost' in *Lord Arthur Savile's Crime & Other Stories* (James R. Osgood, McIlvaine & Co., 1891)

Chapter 11

1. William James, '1896 Society for Psychical Research Presidential Address', reprinted in *Subtle Energies and Energy Medicine*, vol. 7, no. 1 (1996), pp. 23–33
2. William Roll, 'Memory and the long body', in *Research in Parapsychology* (Scarecrow Press, 1989)

Chapter 13

1. See www.noetic.org/about
2. 'They laughed at Galileo too', *New York Times*, 11 August 1996
3. Richard Feynman famously made this remark during his Messenger Lectures at Cornell University (1964). Available at: https://www.youtube.com/watch?v=w3ZRLllWgHI

Chapter 16

1. Alan Heuser (ed.), *Selected Prose of Louis MacNeice* (Clarendon Press, 1990)
2. William Butler Yeats, *A Vision* (Macmillan, 1938)
3. Shani Agron, et al., 'A chemical signal in human female tears lowers aggression in males', *PLOS Biology*, vol. 21 (December 2023). Available at: https://journals.plos.org/plosbiology/article?id=10.1371/journal.pbio.3002442
4. 'Chemical emitted by babies could make men more docile, women more aggressive', Science.org, 19 November 2021
5. 'Autism and the smell of fear', *Weizmann Magazine*, 13 March 2018

Chapter 17

1. Anonymous, 'Battle of Brunanburh', *Anglo-Saxon Chronicle*, after 937 CE
2. Ronald Stewart-Brown, *The Wapentake of Wirral* (Henry Young & Sons, 1907)

Chapter 18

1. G. Hacker et al., 'Geopathic stress zones and their influence on the human organism', in *Spiral Traverse: Journey into the Unknown*, ed. Konstantin Korotkov (2011)

2. Linda Furter, *Geopathische Störzonen und ihre Auswirkungen auf die Gesundheit von Milchkühen* (Dissertation, University of Zurich, 2010)

3. 'Magnetic crystals, guides for animals, found in humans', *New York Times*, 12 May 1992. Available at: https://www.nytimes.com/1992/05/12/science/magnetic-crystals-guides-for-animals-found-in-humans.html

4. 'Can humans sense magnetic fields?', *The Scientist*, 19 May 2019. Available at: https://www.the-scientist.com/can-humans-sense-the-magnetic-field--65611

Chapter 19

1. Hansard, HC (series 5) vol. 746, cols. 99–110 (26 April 2024)

Chapter 21

1. 'Walthamstow: Introduction and domestic buildings', in *A History of the County of Essex: Volume 6* (1973). Available at: https://www.british-history.ac.uk/vch/essex/vol6/pp240-250

2. *Hackney and Islington Gazette*, 1 August 1887

3. These are not the true names of those who lived in this house, but all the facts are. For the sake of privacy and discretion, I've chosen new surnames in the spirit of the Happy Families card game.

Chapter 23

1. Walter Isaacson, *Einstein: His Life and Universe* (Simon & Schuster, 2007)

2. This is an old physics gag often attributed to Einstein, although I could find no substantive evidence that he ever actually said it. More likely, it's just an old joke that's bounced about university lecture theatres for decades, its provenance now lost in the mists of its own subject matter. The earliest printed version of the phrase that I could find was in Ray Cummings' 1922 story *The Girl in the Golden Atom*. Others who have riffed on it, but not claimed credit, include the science-fiction giant Arthur C. Clarke (in *Profiles of the Future*,

1962) and the essayist Susan Sontag (in *At The Same Time: Essays and Speeches*, 2007)

Chapter 24

1. 'The average person walks past 36 murderers in their lifetime – here's how to spot them', *New York Post*, 5 May 2023